HOI

NEW

YOUR SWISS GERMAN SURVIVAL GUIDE

Bergli is being supported by the Swiss Federal Office of Culture with a structural grant for the years 2021–2025.

ISBN 978-3-905252-67-5

Hoi

your new Swiss German survival guide

Fifth edition, 2022
First edition, 2005

Printed in the Czech Republic

www.bergli.ch

HOI

YOUR *NEW* SWISS GERMAN SURVIVAL GUIDE

Written by

Nicole Egger & Sergio J. Lievano

Illustrated & Designed by

Sergio J. Lievano

Table of Contents

Preface to the new edition

When we teamed up for the first edition of *Hoi*, almost twenty years ago, we had no idea what was in store. Now with four language versions, 11 reprintings, and more than 50,000 copies sold (and now an accompanying Illustrated Dictionary!), we have come to grasp how hungry people are for a fun way to learn this crazy and wonderful language. We hope this new version will continue to delight both the newcomer and those who have been struggling with the language for many years.

Swiss German is not one language, but the name given to the group of Alemannic dialects spoken within Switzerland. These dialects (their vocabulary, intonation and pronunciation) vary considerably from one neighbourhood to another. It is a spoken language, and there are contradictory spelling systems for the few occasions when it is written. *Hoi – your Swiss German survival guide* is based primarily on the dialect spoken in the Zurich area, which is spoken by more Swiss than the Swiss dialects spoken in Basel, Berne, Lucerne and other areas. Although the dialects vary in pronunciation and vocabulary, the Swiss usually understand dialects other than their own. This book will help you to do that, too.

Even though Swiss German is not written or standardized and has so many varieties, speakers of Swiss German from all levels of society are proud to speak it. Sharing a language that has so many variations keeps Swiss hearts and souls united.

Part I

About
Swiss German

Introduction to Swiss German

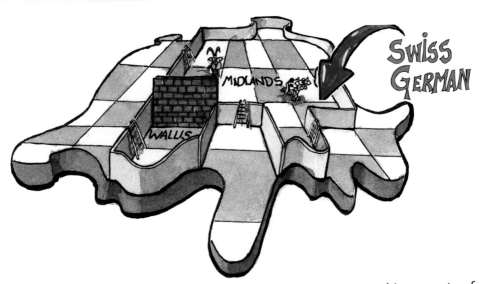

Swiss German, the language spoken in the German-speaking part of Switzerland, is different from the Standard German or High German spoken in Germany. The varieties of Swiss German dialect in Switzerland cannot be defined so easily. No particular dialect is considered better than others. Speaking dialect is not considered 'uneducated' or 'substandard' compared to the written High German but is spoken proudly. A Swiss can identify where another Swiss grew up simply from the dialect spoken.

Identity

For a Swiss German speaker, language is much more than a way of communication; it is an integral part of his/her national, regional and even personal identity.

It is said that each Swiss valley has its own dialect. This is not an exaggeration. Mountains and other geographical barriers have enabled some dialects to develop and keep unique expressions. Some dialects, such as the ones spoken in the Swiss Midlands, have intermingled.

Dialäktgmisch

The interaction of speakers of different dialects has made the peculiarities of some dialects less prevalent. The increasing mobility of the Swiss accelerates this process and leads to a **'Dialäktgmisch'** – a mixture of different dialects.

Brief history of the dialects

Although Switzerland is considered a
multilingual country, it did not start like that.
Back in 1291 when Switzerland was created, the
people founding it all spoke a dialect of Alemannic, a branch
of Upper German covering what is now the south of Germany, Switzerland
and Austria.

Alemannic tribes settled in Switzerland after the fall of the Roman Empire
in the 5th century. These tribes settled predominantly along the Rhine and
in the central and north-eastern regions. Alemannic evolved from this time
into three major groups: 'Low', 'High' and 'Highest' Alemannic. These are not
qualitative terms in any way. These are the geographical terms describing
where the dialect is spoken. The 'Low', located in the Basel area; the 'High',
in the vast majority of regions in Switzerland, and the 'Highest' Alemannic,
found in the remote area of the Wallis.

At the beginning of the 20th century, linguists thought Swiss German would
disappear by the end of the century and that the standard High German of
Germany would prevail in the German-speaking part of Switzerland.

However, the radical political events during this time and the growth of nationalism helped the Swiss retain their dialect as a form of national identity. During the 1930s the Swiss felt the need to distinguish themselves from the Germans, and speaking in Swiss dialect was a way of expressing Swiss patriotism.

Swiss German has reached a new level of acceptance, and continues to gain recognition and popularity, especially among the young, who like hearing it in Swiss popular music and who even compose written forms of it in their e-mail and SMS messages.

There have been many efforts to agree upon a consolidation of the main dialects into a standard Swiss German that could be written. Some rules exist, but the Swiss enjoy their diversity too much to agree on a unified Swiss German. Nevertheless, the use and popularity of Swiss German is steadily increasing in Switzerland.

The Swiss German code

Although it is not well documented, it has been said on many occasions that throughout history, Swiss German dialects were sometimes used as a 'secret coding system' by people and institutions dealing directly or indirectly in political affairs.

The use of High German in Switzerland

Switzerland has what is defined as a **'Diglossia'**: a situation in a society where two languages are used which are closely related and functionally complementary. In the Swiss case, Swiss German is the spoken language, and High German, as the Swiss term **'Schriftdeutsch'** defines it, is the official written language. High German is widely used in the written and spoken media, at schools, and also in the official, social, political or religious events where French-speaking Swiss, Italian-speaking Swiss and other non Swiss-German speakers might be present. Swiss German, on the other hand, is spoken in everyday, informal situations while shopping or socializing with friends and family, in local and regional radio and TV programs, in kindergartens, local government and non-government institutions.

Having Diglossia sometimes makes it difficult to know which language is most appropriate to speak – High German or the dialect. Since High German is their second language, Swiss German speakers are often reluctant to speak High German which does not always make it easy for them to communicate.

High German and Swiss German

Swiss German has 'throaty' or guttural 'ch' and 'k' sounds. The intonation of Swiss German gives emphasis to the first syllable and pitch is more melodious than High German.

Swiss German speakers like to make every possible noun diminutive by placing the ending **'–li'** on it; for example, **Gipfeli** (croissant), **Brötli** (bread roll), **Schäzzli** (sweetheart), **Chäzzli** (little cat), etc.

Swiss German is also very receptive to the influences of foreign languages, in particular to English and French. Due to its geographical and cultural proximity to France, Swiss German has acquired a lot of French vocabulary, as opposed to how foreign words are 'Germanized' in Germany or Austria. The following table shows some examples of French influences on Swiss German:

Swiss German (parenthesis shows pronounciation)	High German	English
Merci (Märsi)	Danke	thank you
s Velo (Welo)	das Fahrrad	bicycle
dä Coiffeur (Guafför)	der Frisör	hairdresser
s Poulet (Pule)	das Hähnchen	chicken
s Cheminée (Schmine)	der Kamin	fireplace
s Spital (Schpital)	das Krankenhaus	hospital
dä Kondukteur (Kondiktör)	der Schaffner	train conductor
s Lavabo (Lawabo)	das Waschbecken	sink
dä Dessert (Dessär)	der Nachtisch	dessert
d' Saison (Säson)	die Jahreszeit	season

The four High German cases of nominative, accusative, dative and genitive are reduced in Swiss German to only two: the 'common case', which covers the German accusative and the nominative; and the 'dative case', which does likewise for the dative and the genitive. (See the Pronouns and Articles Section in the Appendix)

There are also certain misconceptions about Swiss German, due mainly to the fact that it is a spoken rather than a written language. Some people claim an absence of tenses, a lack of gender and of articles. Swiss German does, most certainly, have its own particular tenses (see the Verbs Section in the Appendix), it usually has the same genders as in High German, and it uses articles, even though these, as in most spoken languages, are abbreviated at a conversational level (see table on previous page).

The main differences between Swiss German and High German are related to vocabulary and pronunciation (intonation). Swiss dialects keep their unique, special terms and usually keep the original pronunciation of foreign words that are always creeping into the language.

GERMAN SENTENCE CONSTRUCTION

Translation: Hey! Someone stole your bike!

Use of Swiss German

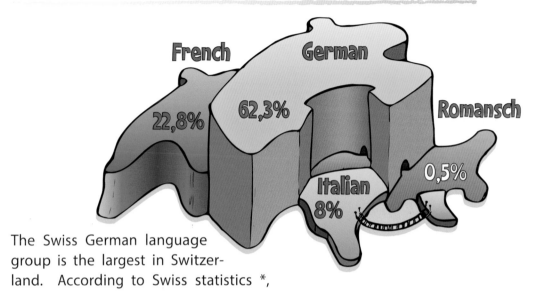

The Swiss German language group is the largest in Switzerland. According to Swiss statistics *, 62,3% of the Swiss population speak this language in their daily lives, followed by French with 22,8%, Italian with 8%, and Romansch (a language with four dialects that was officially recognized only in the 1930s) with 0.5% or 35,000 people.

The diversity of languages and their uneven distribution generate political and social discussions. The **'Röschtigraben'** (fried–potato trench) is the name given to the ideological and linguistic border between the Swiss German and the French speaking area. It is not that there is any real conflict on this imaginary border. The relationship between neighbours is cordial and there is no hate or bitterness (other than the occasional reciprocal jokes). The Röschtigraben term – a kind of potato tortilla that originated in the German speaking part of Switzerland – denotes a different mind set between the two language groups, which is usually highlighted in the political arena.

The Swiss spare no effort to smooth out differences whenever possible, and equalize distribution of power and influence. The federalist form of government helps people living in Switzerland to maintain and respect regional and local distinctions.

*Source: Swiss Federal Statistical Office – Structural survey (2020)

The table on this page shows the multilingual environment where Swiss German is thriving. The large number of non-Swiss, who account for nearly one fifth of the Swiss population, plays an important role in the development of Swiss German. New Swiss generations come not only from Swiss families, but from a mixture of different nationalities and cultural backgrounds. These children of immigrants are called **'Secondos'**. They may have little or no identity with their parents' original country and yet not be considered Swiss either.

Other languages are*:

English	5,8 %
Portuguese	3,5 %
Albanian	3,2 %
Spanish	2,4 %
Serbian, Croatian	2,3 %
Other languages	8,2 %

> HOWCOME, IF I'M
> THE FIRST ONE IN MY
> CLASS, PEOPLE KEEP
> CALLING ME "SECONDO"?

The 'Secondos'...

a term that implies the second generation – act as a bridge of communication between their older relatives and Swiss people and add many new flavours to Swiss German.

Global influences

Young Swiss are of course also influenced by foreign music, foreign fashion, travel and the media, and are always adding new expressions to Swiss German. Like in other countries, Swiss youngsters create their own language identities, separating themselves from older generations.

Why the Swiss don't like to speak High German

ALL I DID WAS ASK IF HE COULD SPEAK HIGH GERMAN...

Many foreigners who learn to speak High German complain that Swiss people only reluctantly reply in High German. Apparently Swiss people generally don't like to speak High German. Why is that so?

For the Swiss, High German is a foreign language. The Swiss prefer to speak their Swiss dialect even though High German is the official German language in Switzerland. High German is the language of school and the language of rules and regulations, but it is rarely associated with pleasure and leisure. On top of this, High German is even for school teachers a foreign language, meaning that they, too, speak a 'helvetic' kind of High German. A lot of Swiss people lack confidence in speaking High German and feel awkward using it.

Although the size and economic power of Germany may sometimes seem threatening to them, a lot of Swiss people are reluctant to speak High German because they feel language-wise in an inferior position rather than because of any animosity towards Germany.

For Swiss people it is particularly unpleasant to speak High German in the company of other Swiss. First they think of this as 'putting on airs' and second they fear making a fool of themselves in front of other Swiss.

Part II

Survival Kit

Consonants

BE AWARE... Since Swiss German is mainly an oral language, this book will keep spelling rules as simple as possible. Therefore we do not use typical German spelling conventions such as **ck, tz, ieh, ah, oh,** etc. The only ones we kept are the v, that has the same pronunciation as f, and dt which is pronounced as t. Instead of **ck**, we used **kk**, for **tz** we used **zz** if the preceding vowel is short.

TIP... Read the Swiss German words out loud as you go through this book. A Swiss Geman speaker also has to do this since the dialect is usually not written.

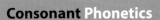

Consonant Phonetics

b   as in **B**lues

ch as in Lo**ch** Ness or Ba**ch**, always voiceless at the back of the throat

d   as in **D**oor

dt 't' as in Le**t**

f   as in **F**inger

g   as in **G**od

gg short strong g (gk) as in French Ja**cqu**es

h   as in **H**ip-**H**op

j   as in **J**es

k   throat rasping **Kh**

l   as in **L**ion

m   as in **M**e

n   as in **N**ight

ng as in English Si**ng**

nk ngk as in Thi**nk**

o   as in **O**lympics

p   as in **P**izza (never aspirated)

qu as in **Qu**antity

r   as in Bu**rr**ito (usually rolled like in Spanish)

s   as in **S**ad (voiceless)

t   as in French **T**u (rather soft, never aspirated)

v   'f' as in **F**inger

w   'v' as in **V**alentine

x   'gs' as in Me**x**ico

z   'ts' as in Lo**ts**

Double consonants are preceded by a short vowel.

Vowels

Vowel Phonetics

a	as in **A**frica	**u**	as in C**oo**l / M**oo**n
ä	as in B**ear**	**ü**	as in French **Tu**
ai	as in **Eye**	**y**	as in French **Tu** (except
au	as in H**ow**		for English words)
e	as in **E**lephant		
ei	as in Hey	**Double vowels** double the
i	as in **Eas**y	length of the sound.
o	as in **O**racle	
ö	as in French D**eux**	

GRAMMAR Swiss phonetics are one of the most complex subjects to discuss. As mentioned in the first part of the book, there are no standard rules and the sounds of letters and words vary from one area to the other. This book gives an approximation of the standard way Swiss German is pronounced in the Zurich region. For more about the dialect spoken in the Basel area, please see our *Sali zämme - your Baseldütsch survival guide.*

BE AWARE... To help you understand Swiss pronunciation of foreign words, a phonetic pronunciation is given in parenthesis.

LEDÄLÄ ?
LEDELE ?
LADELÄ ?
LÄDÄLE ?
...
/ *

* LÄDÄLÄ : TO GO SHOPPING

Greetings & Socializing

Introduction

Formal and Informal

Swiss German differentiates between the formal and the informal way of approaching a person. The formal way uses the pronoun **'Sii'** and the person is usually addressed by his / her last name ('Good morning, Mr. Meier), the informal way is used with the pronoun **'du'** and the person can be addressed by his/her first name ('Hi Chris...').

Grüezi !

Saying Hello (Formal)

Good morning, Mr. / Mrs.	Guätä Morgä Herr / Frau...
	Guätä Tag
Good afternoon.	Guätä Namittag.
Good evening.	Guätä n'Aabig.
Hello.	Grüezi.
Hello. (to several people)	Grüezi mitenand.
How are you?	Wiä gat's Inä?
Fine, and you?	Guät, und Inä?
Pleased to meet you.	Froit mich, Sii kännä z'lärnä.
'Bye.	Uf widerluägä.
	Uf widersee.
	Adieu *(Adjö)*

Formal (Sii)

To be used in business, with strangers, with seniors, or whenever you meet a grown-up that hasn't introduced him / herself with his / her first name. Usually the older, more senior, person offers the **'du'** form **(Sii chönd du zu mir sägä)** or 'wämmer Duzis machä?'

20

BE AWARE... In this book the abbreviation **(inf)** is used for **informal** and **(fr)** is used for **formal**. For nouns: **(m)** is **masculine**, **(f)** is **feminine**, **(n)** is **neutral** and **(pl)** is **plural**.

Saying Hello (Informal)

Hi.	Hoi. / Sali. / Salü.
Hi. (to several people)	Hoi zäme.
How are you?	Wiä gat's? Wiä häsch äs?
Fine, and you?	Guät, und dir?
Quite OK.	Scho rächt.
I am not so well.	Mir gat's nöd so guät.
'Bye.	Ciao. (tschau) / Tschüss.
See you.	Mer gseet sich!
Pleased to meet you.	Froit mich, di kännä z'lärnä.
See you later.	Bis schpöter.
Have a nice day / evening.	No än schönä Tag / Aabig.

Informal: (du / ier)

Usually used with children, friends, family, and among students and colleagues.

Greetings & Socializing

Understanding the language

CHF. 🤚👁️🐦📞 , bitte !

Do you speak English?	Chönd Sii Änglisch? (fr)
	Chasch Änglisch? (inf)
Sorry, I don't understand.	Sorry, ich verschtaa Sii nöd. (fr)
	Sorry, ich verschtaa di nöd. (inf)
What did you say?	Was händ Sii gsait? (fr)
	Was häsch gsait? (inf)
Can you repeat what you said?	Chönd Sii bitte widerholä, was Sii gsait händ? (fr)
	Chasch nomal sägä, was gsait häsch? (inf)
Could you write it down?	Chönted Sii mir das ufschriibä? (fr)
	Chasch mir das ufschriibä? (inf)
Can you say it again slowly?	Chönd Sii das nomal langsam sägä? (fr)
	Chasch das nomal langsam sägä? (inf)
I don't speak Swiss German.	Ich cha kai Schwiizerdütsch.

TIP... **Chönä** is used for both ability and politeness (are you able to? / could you?). In the formal question, the form is '**Chönd Sii?**'; the informal question is '**Chasch?**'. For verb conjugation in Swiss German, check the tables in the Appendix at the end of the book.

 **WARNING !**

Being Polite

In Switzerland (as in many other countries) a golden rule for good communication and understanding is to be polite. Therefore the following words may be very useful when meeting people:

Please.	Bitte.
Thank you.	Danke. / Merci. *(märsi)*
Thanks a lot.	Danke villmal.
Excuse me.	Entschuldigung. / Exgüsi.
May I?	Chönt ich?
	Törf ich?
Yes, please.	Ja, bitte.
No, thank you.	Nai, danke.
I am sorry.	(Äs) tuät mir Laid.
You are welcome.	Bitte, gärn gschee.
You are very kind.	Sii sind seer nätt. (fr)
	Sii sind seer hilfsberait. (fr)
	Du bisch seer nätt. (inf)
	Du bisch seer hilfsberait. (inf)
Would you mind…?	Chönted Sii bitte…? (fr)
	Chöntisch bitte…? (inf)

Questions

TIP.. There are two types of questions:

1. For open questions, where the potential answers are unlimited, the question always starts with a question word (also called w-word) **Wo woonsch?** (Where do you live?), **Was isch dini Liäblingsmusig?** (What's your favourite music?)

2. For closed questions, where the answer is either yes or no, there is no special question word. The question starts with a verb and then the subject: **Chasch (du) Dütsch?** (Do you speak German?) **Schaffsch (du) in Züri?** (Do you work in Zürich?)

Why?
Warum?

When?
Wänn?

What ?
Was ?

How?
Wiä?

Where?
Wo?

How many?
Wiä vill ?

Who?
Wär?

How long?
Wiä lang?

To where.?
Wohi? /
woannä ?

From where?
Vo wo?

Who with?
Mit wäm?

How much?
Wiä vill?

What for?
Warum?/ Für
was?

Greetings & Socializing

Small talk

Introducing Yourself

What is your name?	Wiä isch Irä Namä? (fr)
	Wiä haissed Sii? (fr)
	Wiä isch din Namä? (inf)
	Wiä haissisch? (inf)
My name is...	Ich haissä...
Where are you from?	Wohär chömed Sii? (fr)
	Wohär chunnsch du? (inf)
I come from...	Ich chumä us...
Where do you live?	Wo woned Sii? (fr)
	Wo wonsch? (inf)
I live in...	Ich wonä in...
How long have you been here?	Wiä lang sind Sii scho da? (fr)
	Wiä lang bisch scho da? (inf)
I have been here for...years.	Ich bi scho....Jaar da.
What do you do in your spare time?	Was mached Sii i Irerä Freiziit? (fr)
	Was machsch i dinerä Freiziit? (inf)
I like...	Ich ha... gärn
I love...	Ich liäbä...
I'm interested in...	Ich interessierä mich für...

TIP... Swiss German is a so- called 'pro drop' language, which means the subject can be left out, but only in the first and second person singular. One can say: **Ich chumä**, or just **chumä** (the second being more colloquial).

Greetings & Socializing

 **WARNING !** The Swiss German word **'ledig'** means 'Not married'. The English word **'single'** is also used in Swiss German, but it only means 'with no boyfriend / girlfriend' (not in a relationship). So one can be 'ledig' but not 'single', meaning one lives with somebody without being married.

Getting Personal

Are you married?	Sind Sii ghüratä? (fr)
	Sind Sii verhüratet? (fr)
	Bisch ghüratä? (inf)
	Bisch verhüratet? (inf)
Are you single?	Sind Sii single? (fr)
	Bisch single? (inf)
Do you have a boy / girlfriend?	Händ Sii än Fründ / ä Fründin? (fr)
	Häsch än Fründ / ä Fründin? (inf)
Do you have children?	Händ Sii Chind? (fr)
	Häsch Chind? (inf)
How is your family?	Wiä gat's Irerä Familiä? (fr)
	Wiä gat's dinerä Familiä? (inf)
What's your telephone number?	Wiä isch Iri Telefonnummerä? (fr)
	Wiä isch dini Telefonnummerä?(inf)
My number is...	Mini Nummerä isch...
I don't have an e-mail address.	Ich ha kai Emailadrässä.
What's your address?	Wiä isch Iri Adrässä? (fr)
	Wiä isch dini Adrässä? (inf)
Which street?	A wellärä Schtrass?

First Approach

Do you want to go and have a drink?	Wänd Sii ais go ziä? (fr)
	Wänd Sii öppis go trinkä? (fr)
	Wotsch ais go ziä? (inf)
	Wotsch öppis go trinkä? (inf)
Can I invite you for a drink?	Chann ich Inä än Drink schpendierä? (fr)
	Chann ich dir än Drink schpendierä? (inf)
Do you want to come with me / us ?	Chunnsch mit mir / ois?
Are you coming?	Chömed Sii? (fr) / Chunnsch? (inf)
Let's go somewhere.	Gömmer noimät anä.
Do I know you from somewhere?	Känn ich Sii vo noimät?(fr) / Känned mir
ois?	
	Känn ich di vo noimät? (inf)
Do you want to dance?	Wänd Sii tanzä?(fr)
	Wotsch tanzä? (inf)
Do you have a cigarette?	Händ Sii ä Zigarettä? (fr)
	Häsch ä Zigi? (inf)

Negative Answers

No, I don't smoke.	Nai, ich rauchä nöd.
I have to go now.	Ich muäs jezt gaa.
Please, leave me alone!	Lönd Sii mich bitte in Ruä! (fr)
	La mich bitte in Ruä! (inf)
Get lost!	Hau ab! (inf) / Haued Sii ab! (fr)
I don't think so.	Ich glaub nöd.
I want to go home.	Ich möcht hai.
I need to go home.	Ich muäs hai.
I have to work tomorrow.	Ich muäs morn schaffä.
I have no time.	Ich ha kai Ziit.
I don't have any money.	Ich ha kai Gäld.
I don't feel like.	Ich ha kai Luscht.

Greetings & Socializing

Invitations

Key Survival Phrases

May I invite you for dinner tomorrow night?
Törf ich Sii morn aabig zum Ässä iiladä?(fr)
Törf ich di morn aabig zum Ässä iiladä? (inf)

Yes, I would love to come. Ja, ich chumä gärn.

Thank you for the invitation. Danke für d'liladig.

to be on time pünktlich sii

to be late verschpötet sii

Sorry for being late. Entschuldigung für d'Verschpötig.

The food is delicious. S'Ässä isch seer fain / s'Ässä schmökkt wunderbar.

Please bring your partner. Sii chönd gärn Irä Partner / Iri Partnerin mitbringä. (fr)
Du chasch gärn din Fründ / dini Fründin mitnää. (inf)

No, I am sorry, but I have another appointment.
Tuät mir Laid, da chani nöd. Ich ha dänn scho öppis vor.

TIP... In Switzerland, people usually bring something to a party. The most common gifts are wine, sweets or flowers. When invited to a barbecue or an informal party, it is polite to offer to bring something: **Chann ich öppis mitbringä?** (Can I bring something?)

➕ Common Swiss Events ➕

Party	Party (f) *(Parti)*
	Fäscht (n)
Birthday party	Geburtstags-party (f)
Barbecue	Grillfäscht (n)
Farewell party	Apschidsfäscht (n)
Brunch	Brunch (m)
Lunch	Zmittagässä (n)
Dinner	Znacht (m)
	Znachtässä (n)
Coffee party	Kafiklatsch (m)
	Kafichränzli (n)
Hen night / Stag night	Polteraabig (m)
Housewarming party	Husiweiigs-party (f)

Love

TIP... The Swiss are keen on pet names, the most common of which are:

Schäzzli (little treasure), **Tübli** (little dove), **Müüsli** (little mouse), **Chäferli** (little beetle), **Schnugi** (sweetie), **Bärli** (little bear).

Key Survival Phrases (informal)

to love	liäbä
I love you.	Ich liäbä di / Ich ha di gärn. *(see Tip p.30)*
I need you.	Ich bruchä di.
I miss you.	Ich vermissä di.
You are very pretty / sexy.	Du bisch mega / seer hübsch / sexy.
You are the love of my life.	Du bisch d'Liäbi vo mim Läbä.
Kiss me.	Küss mich.
I've fallen in love with you.	Ich ha mich i di verliäbt.
We fell in love.	Mir händ ois verliäbt.
I am in love.	Ich bi verliäbt.
Let's move in / live together.	Chumm mir ziänd zäme.
You make me very happy.	Du machsch mich total / mega happy.
She is my girlfriend.	Sii isch mini Fründin.
He is my boyfriend.	Er isch min Fründ.
We are just friends.	Mir sind nur Kollegä.
We love each other.	Mir liäbed ois.
I like her / him.	Er / Sii gfallt mir.
Love at first sight.	Liäbi uf dä erschti Blikk.
We first met in...	Mit händ ois in...kän glärnt.
Partner	Partner (m) / Partnerin (f)
	Läbäspartner (m) / Läbäspartnerin (f)
to get to know each other	sich kännä lernä

TIP... 'Ich ha di gärn' (I like you) may be understood romantically, but not necessarily. 'Ich liäbä di,' (I love you) on the other hand, is strong and is mainly used in a romantic context and not between friends.

BE AWARE... In Swiss German, the words 'Fründ (m)' and 'Fründin (f)' refer to a friend, as well as a boyfriend or girlfriend.

When the Swiss want to make it clear that somebody is their boyfriend or girlfriend, they may say: **min Fründ** (my friend) for boyfriend or **mini Fründin** for girlfriend. **Än Fründ (m)** or **ä Fründin (f),** on the other hand, is just a friend.

The word **'Kolleg'** is also used for friends, including friends outside work that aren't colleagues in the English sense.

WARNING !

Many mistakes are made just by the wrong usage of the preposition that comes together with the verb. In order not to jeopardise good communication keep in mind the following:

bim John / bi dä Anna schlafä
Sleep at John's / Anna's place

näbäd äm John / näbäd dä Anna schlafä
Sleep next to John / Anna

mit äm John / mit dä Anna schlafä
Sleep with John / Anna (to have sex).

Sexual Preferences

I like women.	Ich schtaa uf Frauä.
I like men.	Ich schtaa uf Manä.
heterosexual	hetero(sexuell)
homosexual	homo(sexuell)
gay	schwul
lesbian	lesbisch

Greetings & Socializing

Wedding Stuff

to get engaged	sich verlobä *
I got engaged.	Ich ha mich verlobt.
to get married	hüratä
to be married	ghüratä sii
I am married.	Ich bi ghüratä.
Marriage	Ehe (f)
Wedding	Hochziit (f)
We are getting married.	Mir hüratet.
Wedding eve's party	Polteraabig (m)
Do you want to marry me?	Möchtisch mich hüratä? (inf)
	Möchtisch mini Frau / min Maa werdä? (inf)
Yes, I do.	Ja, ich will.
No, I don't want to / yet.	Nai, ich möcht nöd / nonig.

GRAMMAR

* Sich verlobä / sich verliäbä are reflexive verbs. Reflexive verbs have the following conjugation:

ich verliäbä mich
du verliäbsch di
er/sii verliäbt sich
mir verliäbed ois
ier verliäbed oi
sii verliäbed sich

31

Loveless (informal)

There is someone else.	Ich ha än anderä (m) / än anderi. (f)
I hate you.	Ich hassä di.
Let's take a break.	Chumm, mir mached ä Pausä.
Have you been unfaithful?	Häsch du mich betrogä?
We are just friends.	Mir sind nur Kollegä.
I am not in love.	Ich bi nöd verliäbt.
to move out	uusziä
S/he moved out.	Sii/Er isch uszogä.
to have an affair	än Affärä ha
to betray somebody	öpper betrügä
S/he betrayed me.	Sii/Er hätt mich betrogä.
Argument	Schtriit (m)
argue	schtriitä
to separate	sich tränä
to get a divorce	sich schaidä la
divorced	gschidä
to hate each other	sich hassä

GRAMMAR

Sich schaidä la is an expression that is used in the following way:

Ich la mich schaidä.
(I am getting a divorce)
Ich will mich schaidä la.
(I want to get a divorce)
Sii lönd sich schaidä.
(They are getting a divorce)

...BE A DEAR AND PASS ME THE SALT....

Things to say at special moments

Survival Words and Phrases

Happy Birthday!	Alles Gueti zum Geburtstag!
Merry Christmas!	Schöni Wiänachtä!
Happy New Year!	Äs guäts Nois! / Än guätä Rutsch!
	Äs guäts nois Jaar!
I wish you...	Ich wünschä dir (inf) / Inä (fr)...
Happy Anniversary!	Än guetä Jaarestag! Ä schöns Jubiläum!
Good Luck!	Vill Glükk! / Vill Erfolg!
Best wishes!	Alles Gueti!
Fantastic!	Fantastisch!
Beautiful!	Schön!
Delicious!	So fain!
Welcome!	Willkomä!
Break a leg!	Hals und Baibruch!
Enjoy your meal!	Än Guetä!
Congratulations!	Alles Gueti!
	Ich gratulierä
To your health!	Uf dini Gsundhait!
I wish you success!	Vill Erfolg!
Have a nice trip!	Schöni Rais!
Get well!	Gueti Besserig!
Cheers!	Proscht! / Pröschtli!

Misfortune and Sympathy

Sorry.
Äs tuät mir Laid. / Sorry.

My deepest condolences.
Mis tüfi Biilaid.

I hope you get well soon.
Ich hoffä, äs gat bald besser.

Bad luck
Päch

Better luck next time.
Vill Glükk snächscht Mal.

What a shame!
Schad!

I warned you.
Ich ha di gwarnt.

Work

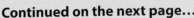

Key Survival Phrases

Do you work?	Sind Sii pruäfstätig? / Schaffed Sii? (fr)
	Bisch pruäfstätig? / Schaffsch? (inf)
What do you do?	Was mached Sii? / Was schaffed Sii?(fr)
	Was machsch? / Was schaffsch? (inf)
What is your profession?	Was isch Irä Pruäf ? (fr)
	Was händ Sii glärnt? (fr)
	Was isch din Pruäf ? (inf)
	Was häsch glärnt? (inf)
I am...	Ich bi...
Where do you work?	Wo schaffed Sii? (fr)
	Wo schaffsch? (inf)
I work at...	Ich schaffä bi...
I work at home.	Ich schaffä dähai.
I work freelance.	Ich bin unäbhängig.
I am not working.	Ich schaffä nöd.
I am employed at...	Ich bin agschtellt bi...
I am unemployed.	Ich bin arbetslos.
I am self-employed.	Ich bi sälbscht-
	schtändig.

Continued on the next page...

Paperwork

Appraisal	Quali(fikation) (f)		
	Laischtigsbewärtig (f)	**Report**	Pricht (m)
Contract	Vertrag (m)	**Minutes**	Protokoll (n)
Form	Formular (n)	**Invoice**	Rächnig (f)
Job application	Bewärbig (f)	**Purchase order**	Pschtellig (f)
Plan	Plan (m)		Uuftrag (m)

TIP... The working environment in Switzerland is probably the most common place where English and Swiss German merge. English remains as the international business language, so the business area names tend to be in English (e.g. **Customer Service, Finance, Procurement, Supply Chain...**).

Work

Key Survival Phrases

have a meeting	Ich hann äs Meeting / ä Sizzig / ä Beschprächig.
We have a problem.	Mir händ äs Problem.
We are successful.	Mir sind seer erfolgriich.
We made ... profit.	Mir händ ... Gwünn gmacht.
We made ... turnover.	Mir händ... Umsazz gmacht.
We made... loss.	Mir händ ... Verluscht gmacht.
We create jobs.	Mir schaffed Arbetspläzz.
You have the job.	Sii händ d'Schtell.
You are fired.	Sii sind entlaa.
I want to resign.	Ich möcht kündigä.
I want a salary raise.	Ich möcht ä Loonerhöig.
Would you have lunch with me?	Chömed Sii mit mir go zmittagässä? (fr)
	Chunnsch mit mir go zmittagässä? (inf)
Could you explain please?	Chönd Sii mir das bitte erchlärä? (fr)
	Chasch mir das erchlärä? (inf)
I want to go on holiday from ...till...	Ich möcht vo....bis.... i d'Feriä.
Could you make a presentation for me?	Chönd Sii mir ä Präsentazion machä? (fr)
	Chasch mir ä Präsentazion machä? (inf)
I would like to discuss something with you.	Ich möcht öppis mit Inä beschprächä. (fr)
	Ich möcht öppis mit dir beschprächä. (inf)

Work

I ONLY TOLD HER MY PLANS TO RETURN TO WORK AS SOON AS THE BABY IS BORN...

Payment

Payment	Zalig (f)
Bonus	Bonus (m)
Salary	Loon (m)
	Salär (n)
Fee	Gebür (f)
	Priis (m)
Overtime	Überschtundä (pl)
Commission	Komission (f)
Costs	Choschtä (pl)
Pension fund	Pensionskassä (f)
Discounts	Verbilligung (f)
Insurance	Versicherig (f)
Taxes	Schtürä (pl)
Part time	tailziit
Full time	vollziit

Time @ Work

Appointment	Termin (m)
Break	Pausä (f)
Coffee break	Kafipausä (f)
Conference	Konfäränz (f)
Job interview	Bewärbigsgschpräch (n)
Vacations	Feriä (pl)
Presentation	Präsentazion (f)
Course	Kurs (m)
Lunch break	Mittagspausä (f)
Meeting	Beschprächig (f)
	Sizzig (f)
	Meeting (n) *(miiting)*

Working Areas

Smoking area	Rauchereggä (m)
Office	Gschäft (n)
	Büro (n)
Canteen	Kantinä (f)
	Mensa (f)
Warehouse	Lagerhallä (f)
	Warähuus (n)
Reception	Empfang (m)
Studio	Schtudio (n)
Garage	Garage (f) *(Garasch)*
Parking area	Parkplazz (m)
Laboratory	Labor (n)

Dress Code

Dress Code	Chlaidervorschrift (f)	Uniform	Uniform (f)
Business casual	unzwungä	Briefcase	Arbetsmappä (f)
Suit	Aazug (m)	Dress	Chlaid (n)
Tie	Grawattä (f)		

Job Title

Board of Directors	Verwaltigsrat (m)	**Worker**	Arbaiter (m)
Boss	Chef (m) *(Schef)*	**Worker**	Arbaiterin (f)
	Chefin (f) *(Schefin)*	**Trainee**	Praktikant (m)
Employer	Arbetgeber (m)		Praktikantin (f)
	Arbetgeberin (f)	**Customer**	Chund (m)
Employee	Agschtellte (m)		Chundin (f)
	Agschtellti (f)	**Occupation**	Job (m) *(Tschop)*
Colleague	Arbetskolleg (m)		Pruäf (m)
	Arbetskollegin (f)	**Job description**	Jobbeschribig (f)
Director	Diräktor (m)	**Secretary**	Sekretär/in (m/f)
	Diräktorin (f)		Sekretär (m)
Manager	Manager (m)	**Assistant**	Asischtänt (m)
	(Mänätscher)		Asischtäntin (f)
	Managerin (f)	**Technician**	Techniker (m)
	(Mänätscherin)		Technikerin (f)
Partner	Partner (m)	**Consultant**	Berater (m)
	Partnerin (f)		Beraterin (f)
Professional	Profi (m)	**Cleaner**	Puzzma (m)
Owner	Psizzer (m)		Puzzfrau (f)
	Psizzerin (f)	**Receptionist**	Resepzionischt (m)
Salesperson	Verchoiffer (m)		Resepzionischtin (f)
Salesperson	Verchoifferin (f)	**Apprentice**	Leerling (m)

Telephone and mobile phones

Communication

May I talk to Mr. X / Ms. Y?	Chann ich mit äm Herr X / dä Frau Y redä? (fr)
Could you connect me to Mr. X?	Chönted Sii mich bitte mit äm Härr X verbindä? (fr)
I'll connect you.	Ich verbindä Sii
Can I call you back?	Chann ich Inä zrugglütä? (fr)
	Chann ich dir zrugglütä? (inf)
What are you calling about...?	Um was gat's?

When Calling

...YOUR CALL IS BEING HELD IN A QUEUE. THE WAITING TIME IS CURRENTLY 25 MINUTES. IN THE MEANTIME, LET US INTRODUCE YOU TO OUR NEW PRODUCTS AND SERVICES THAT WILL ENSURE TOTAL CUSTOMER SATISFACTION...

TIP... When answering a phone call, Swiss usually say their full name: **Christa Müller.** When calling, Swiss usually introduce themselves: **Da isch d'Christa Müller. Chönt ich bitte mit äm Herr Meier redä?** (This is Christa Müller speaking. May I talk to Mr. Meier?). A phone conversation is usually ended with: **Uf Widerhörä.**

It is also polite to ask **Stör ich?** (Am I disturbing you?), when calling somebody unexpectedly, or **Händ Sii churz Ziit?** (fr) (Do you have a moment?) at the beginning of a conversation.

Telephone Words

Answering machine	Telefonbeantworter (m)
Area code	Vorwaal (f)
cancel	löschä / känslä
Local call	lokalä Aaruäf (m)
Long distance call	internazionalä Aaruäf (m)
Mobile phone	Händi (n) / Natel (n)
Operator	Vermittlig (f)
Phone call	Aaruäf (m)
Public telephone	öffentlichs Telefon (n)
Telephone bill	Telefonrächnig (f)
Telephone book	Telefonbuäch (n)
Telephone card	Telefonchartä (f)
to telephone / call	aalütä

Key Survival Phrases

Can I use your phone?	Chann ich mal Iräs Telefon benuzzä? (fr)
	Chann ich mal dis Telefon benuzzä? (inf)
I will call you.	Ich lüt Inä aa. (fr) / Ich lüt dir aa. (inf)
There was no answer.	Niämärt hätt abgno.
The line is busy / engaged.	Äs isch psezt.
I want to make a collect call to...	Ich möcht äs R-Gschpröch nach ... machä.
I need to recharge my mobile phone.	Ich muäs mis Natel ufladä.
There is no telephone line.	Äs hätt kai Verbindig.
The phone is ringing.	S'Telefon lütet.
Wrong number.	Falsch verbundä.
How much does a minute cost to...?	Wiä vill choschtet's ä Minutä uf ... z'telefonierä?
Please turn off your mobile phone.	Schtelled Sii bitte Iräs Händi ab. (fr)
	Schtell bitte dis Händi ab. (inf)

Mobile Phone Phrases

Send me your contact details.	Schikked Sii mir Iri Kontaktagabä? (fr)
	Schikksch mir dini Kontaktagabä?(inf)
Do you have a charger?	Händ Sii än Tschartschär? (fr)
	Häsch än Tschartschär? (inf)
I ran out of credit!	Ich ha kai Kredit me.
I'm running out of battery.	Mini Batteriä sind läär.
I scratched my screen.	Min Skriin isch verchrazzt.
I can use the GPS.	Ich cha mis Tschipiäss bruchä.
Which provider do you use?	Bi welläm Abüüter sind Sii? (fr)
	Bi welläm Abüüter bisch? (inf)
I don't have a connection here.	Ich ha da kai Verbindig.
Do you know this app?	Känned Sii diä Äpp? (fr)
	Kännsch diä Äpp? (inf)
I will download this app.	Ich ladä diä Äpp abä.

Mobile Phone Words

App	Äpp (f)	Head phones	Chopfhöörer (m)
Credit	Kredit (m)	Memory card	Schpaicherchartä (f)
Prepaid account	Pri-peid Abo (n).	Photo gallery	Fotigallerii (f)
Network	Nezzwärch (n)	Contacts	Kontäkt (pl)
Wifi connection	Waifai Verbindig (f)	Smart phone	Smart foon (n)
Install	inschtalliärä, iirichtä		

Communication

Computer world

E-mail

Symbol '@'	Affeschwanz (m)	**Laptop**	Laptop (m) *(Läptop)*
Address book	Addrässbuäch (n)	**log in**	iiloggä
Connection	Verbindig (f)	**log out**	uusloggä
copy	kopierä	**reply**	antwortä
Desktop	Desktop (m)		zruggschriibä
Attachment	Attachment (n)	**Subject**	Thema (n)
	(Attätschmänt)	**Trash**	Apfallchorb (m)
forward	forwardä		Apfall (m)
	wiiterlaitä	**E-mail**	E-mail (n)
Text message	SMS (n) (Äsämäs)		Mail (n) *(Meil)*

Key Computer Terms

Printer	Printer (m) / Drukker (m)
print	drukkä
Screen	Bildschirm (m)
open a program	Äs Programm öffnä
save a program	Äs Programm abschpaicherä
burn a CD	Ä CD bränä (Zede)
open a new folder	Än noiä Ordner aleggä
turn on the computer	Dä Computer aaschtelä
turn off the computer	Dä Computer usschaltä
Download	abeladä / downlowdä *(daunloudä)*

Survival E-mail Phrases

I need to check my e-mails.	Ich muäs mal mini Emails aaluägä.
There is no Internet connection.	Äs hätt kai Internetaaschluss.
That is a virus / spam.	Ich hann än Wirus / äs Späm-Mail.
I will e-mail you.	Ich schrib Inä äs Email. (fr)
	Ich maile dir. (inf)
Send me an e-mail.	Schribed Sii mir äs Email bitte. (fr)
	Schrib mer äs Mail. (inf)
I deleted your e-mail.	Ich ha Iräs Mail glöscht. (fr)
	Ich ha dis Mail glöscht. (inf)
Stop sending me e-mails.	Schribed Sii mir kai Mails me. (fr)
	Schrib mer kai Email me (inf)
What's your e-mail?	Was isch Iri Email? (fr)
	Was isch dini Email? (inf)

Communication

HI!... I WOULD LIKE TO BE YOUR ´FRIEND´...

Social Networking

Communication

Social Networking Terms

Tweet	Tweet (m) *(Twiit)*
Facebook	Facebook (n) *(Feisbuk)*
tweeting	Tweetä *(twiitä)*
chatting	tschättä
WhatsApp	WhatsApp (n) *(Wattsäpp)*
app	App (f) *(Äpp)*
wifi	Wifi (n) *(Waifai)*
selfie	Selfie (n) *(Sälfi)*
profile	Profile (n) *(Profail)*
sexting	sextä
poke	aschtuppsä
instagram	Instagram (n) *(Inschtagramm)*
social networking	Social networkä
Skype	Skype (n) *(Skaip)*

Social Networking Phrases

Do you Tweet?	Twiited Sii (fr)? / Twiitisch (inf)?
Let's be friends on Facebook.	Chömed Sii, mir wärded Fründä uf Feisbuk! (fr), Chumm, mir wärded Fründä uf Feisbuk (inf)
Do you have WhatsApp?	Händ Sii Wattsäpp? (fr)/ Häsch Wattsäpp? (inf)
Which one is the app for...?	Welläs isch d'... Äpp?
Is there any wifi here?	Gitt's da Waifai?
What is the access code?	Welläs isch dä Äxess Kod?
I don't have a Facebook account.	Ich bi nöd uf Feisbuk.
I will re-tweet your post.	Ich twiitä Irä Poust (fr) / din Poust (inf) wiiter.
Skype me!	Skaiped Sii mir (fr)!/Skaip mir (inf)!
What's your Skype name?	Welläs isch Irä Skaip-Namä (fr)?/ Welläs ich din Skaip-Namä (inf)?
He/she got caught sexting	Er/si isch bim Sextä verwütscht wordä.
I will unfriend him/her.	Ich strich in (m)/si (f) als Fründ/in.
I will google it!	Ich guuglä das.
How many"likes" have you got?	Wiä vill "laiks" händ Sii scho (fr)?/ Wiä vill "laiks" häsch scho (inf)?

BE AWARE... Swiss dialects tend to play a more important role in social media than in traditional media. Young people in particular use Swiss German not only for SMS and WhatsApp but often for Facebook, Twitter, Instagram, Skype etc... However, official information (e.g. airport announcements) and the sharing of professional documents (e.g. a CV in Linkedin or Xing), are still done in High German.

....AND YOU DEAR... ARE YOU MISSING ME...?

Social Networking Phrases

I am following him/her on twitter.	Ich folgä im (m)/irä (f) uf Twitter.
I saw it on my newsfeed (Facebook).	Ich has uf mim Njusfiid (Feisbuk) gse.
He/She is in my circle (Gmail contacts).	Er (m) /Si (f) ghört zu minä Tschi-Meil-Kontäkt.
Do you mind if I share your post /picture?	Channi Irä Poust/Iräs Foti tailä?/ (fr)
	Channi din Poust/dis Foti tailä? (inf)

PEOPLE ENJOYING "SKYPE"... TRULY THEY'RE NOT UNDERSTANDING ITS FULL POTENTIAL...

...OKAY, AND NOW, KNEEL DOWN..! I NEED TO CHECK UNDER THE SOFA...

Social Networking Phrases

This post went viral.	Dä Poust hätt sich wiral verbreität.
Is there an app for that?	Gitts für das än Äpp?
Someone called me on WhatsApp.	Öpper hätt mir uf Wattsäpp aglütä.

Excuse me, would you mind if I used your Wifi?
Tschuldigung, chann ich Iräs Waifai bruchä? (fr)/
Tschuldigung, chann ich dis Waifai bruchä (inf)?

Yes, someone called me from this mobile phone.
Ja, öpper hätt mir vo derä Nummerä us aglütä.

Can you send me that/those photos to my mobile phone?
Chönd Si mir das Foti/diä Fotenä uf mis Händi schikkä (fr)?
Chasch mir das Foti/diä Fotenä uf mis Händi schikkä (inf)?

I will send you a message on WhatsApp.
Ich schikkä Inä (f)/dir (inf) ä Nachricht uf Wattsäpp.

I like the filter you used on that picture (Instagram).
Mir gfallt dä Filter wo Si (fr)/du (inf) für das Bild uf Inschtagramm brucht
händ (fr)/ häsch (inf).

I blocked his/her comments / I blocked him/her.
Ich ha sini (m)/iri (f) Kommentär blokirt / Ich hann in (m) / si (f) blokiert.

Excuse me, may I use your network to check my e-mails?
Tschuldigung, chann ich Iräs Nezzwärk bruche zum d'Meils tschäggä? (fr) /
Tschuldigung, chann ich dis Nezzwärk bruche zum d'Meils tschäggä? (inf)

Swiss Texting Terms

Abbreviation	Swiss German	English meaning
akla	alles klar?	Everything understood? /All clear?
BPG	bi passender Glegähait	At the right moment
BSE	bin so ainsam	I am so lonely
BVID	bin verliäbt i dich	I am in love with you
cola	chummä schpöter	Will come later
cu(l)	si ju leiter	See you later
DAD	dänk a dich	Thinking of you
DD	drükk dich	Hug you
DGGN	das gaat gar nöd	This doesn't work/not like this
dubido	du bisch doof	You are stupid
ev	eventuell	Maybe
ff	Fortsezzig folgt	To be continued
ggg	ganz gross grins	Very big ..smile
glg	ganz liäbi Grüässli	Warm regards
gn	gaat's no!	Are you crazy?
gn8	guät Nacht	Good night
guk / g&k	Gruäss und Kuss	Regards and kiss
HASE	hann Seensucht	Longing for
hdg	ha di gärn	Love you
hdmfg	ha di mega fescht gärn	Love you very much
IKD	ich küssä dich	Kiss you
ka	kai Aanig	No idea
kp	kain Plan	No plan
lg	liäbi Grüäss(li)	Kind regards
lw	langwilig	Boring
LZS	Luscht z'schribä?	Feel like writing?
MAMIMA	meil mir mal	E-mail me
mfg	mit fründlichä Grüäss	Best regards
NOK	nöd oni Kondom	Not without condom
STIMST	schta im Schtau	I am caught in traffic jam
sz	schrib zrugg	Write back
t+	dänk positiv	Think positive
vlt	villicht	Maybe
WASA	wartä uf schnälli Antwort	Wait for fast replay
Wayne	Wen interessiert's?	Who cares?
ZUMIOZUDI	zu mir oder zu dir?	at my place or your place?

Communication

Post Office

Communication

The Post

Envelope	Couvert (n) *(Kuwäär)*	**Postcard**	Poschtchartä (f)
Address	Adrässä (f)	**Airmail**	Luftposcht (f)
Sender's address	Apsänder/in (m/f)	**Registered letter**	igschribnä Briäf (m)
Post office	Poscht (f)	**Registered mail**	igschribni Poscht (f)
Mail box	Briäfchaschtä (m)	**Postcode**	Poschtlaitzaal (f)
Postman	Pöschtler (m)	**to send**	sändä
	Pöschtlerin (f)		schikkä
Packet	Päkkli (n)	**Stamp**	Markä (f)
Letter	Briäf (m)	**Care of**	zuhandä vo
Postage stamp	Poschtschtämpfel (m)	**Postal money order**	Gäldüberwiisig (f)
Post	Poscht (f)		

Survival Post Phrases

I'd like to send this letter fast delivery.
Ich möcht dä Briäf mit A-Poscht schikkä.

I would like to redirect my post.
Ich möcht mini Poscht umlaitä.

What's the postcode of…?
Was isch d'Poschtlaitzaal vo…?

How much does it cost to send this package high priority?
Wiä vill choschtet's dä Briäf mit A-Poscht z'schikkä?

How can I apply for a P.O. Box?
Wiä chumm ich äs Poschtfach über?

What's the fastest way to send this letter / package?
Wiä chann ich dä Briäf / das Päkkli am schnellschtä schikkä?

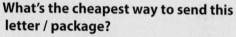

What's the cheapest way to send this letter / package?
Wiä chann ich dä Briäf / das Päkkli am billigschtä schikkä?

When will it arrive?
Wänn chunnt's a?

Can you give me a price list?
Händ Sii mir ä Priislischtä?

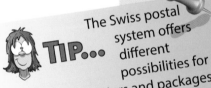

TIP… The Swiss postal system offers different possibilities for sending letters and packages. The most common ones are:

B- Poscht: Low priority delivery. Within Switzerland it usually takes two to three days for letters to be delivered.

A- Poscht: High Priority delivery. Within Switzerland it usually takes one day for letters to be delivered.

Express: Fast Delivery.

ligschriibä: Certified or recorded delivery. It requires a signature from the recipient.

website: www.swisspost.ch

Media (news)

In the News

		Gossip	Klatsch (m)
Advertising	Wärbig (f)		Tratsch (m)
Article	Artikel (m)	**to gossip**	klatschä
Art	Kunscht (f)	**Headlines**	Schlagzilä (pl)
Bulletin board	Aschlagbrätt (n)	**International news**	Ussland-Nachrichtä (pl)
Cable TV	Kabelfernse (n)	**Local news**	lokali Noiigkaitä (pl)
Celebrity	Promi (m)		lokali Nachrichtä (pl)
	VIP (m) *(Wiaipi)*	**Magazine**	Heftli (n)
Channel	Kanal (m)	**Music**	Musig (f)
Culture	Kultur (f)	**National news**	Inland-Nachrichtä (pl)
Editor	Herusgeber (m)		
	Herusgeberin (f)		
Famous	berüämt / bekannt	**Continued on the next page...**	
Fashion	Modä (f)		

In the News

News	Nachrichtä (pl)
Newspaper	Zitig (f)
Obituary	Todesaazaig (f)
Opinion	Mainig (f)
Photo	Foti (n)
Radio	Radio (m)
Satellite	Satellit (m)
Section	Apschnitt (m)
	Tail (m)
Society	Gsellschaft (f)
Sports	Schport (m)
Talk show	Talk Show (f)
	(Tok Schou)
Television	Fernse (n)
Television licence	Fernsebewilligung (f)

Communication

Food and drinks

Key Survival Phrases

I'm hungry.	Ich ha Hunger.
I'm thirsty.	Ich ha Turscht.
A table for two, please.	Än Tisch für zwai, bitte.
Can I see the menu, please?	Händ Sii mir ä Schpiis-chartä bitte?
	Chann ich emal d'Spiis-chartä aluägä, bitte?
would like...	Ich möcht...
with / without spicy sauce	mit scharfer Sosä / ooni scharfi Sosä
with / without lemon	mit / ooni Zitrone
A little...	Äs bizzeli...
A bottle of mineral water, please.	Ä Fläschä Wasser, bitte
with / without ice...	Mit / ooni Iis
A beer, please / a wheat beer, please.	Ä Schtangä, bitte. / Äs Waizä, bitte.
Can I have the bill, please?	Chann ich zalä, bitte?
Can you split the bill?	Chömmer trännt zalä?
Did you enjoy the meal?	Isch guät gsi? / Isch rächt gsi?
The food was good / bad.	S'Ässä isch guät / nöd so guät gsi.
to take away	zum Mitnää

Meat

Meat	Flaisch (n)
Bacon	Schpäkk (m)
Beef	Rindflaisch (n)
Chicken	Huän (n)
	Poulet (n) *(Pule)*
Ham	Schinkä (m)
Lamb	Lamm (n)
Liver	Läbere (f)
Pork	Schwinigs (n)
	Schwaineflaisch (n)
Salami	Salami (m)
Sausage	Wurscht (f)
Steak	Steak (n) *(Steik)*
Turkey	Truthaan (m)
Veal	Chalbflaisch (n)

Meals

Meals	Maalzitä (pl)
Starter	Vorschpiis (f)
Cocktail	Aperitif (m)
Breakfast	Zmorgä (m)
Dessert	Dessert (m) *(Dessär)*
Dinner / Supper	Znacht (m)
Lunch	Zmittag (m)
Main course	Hauptschpiis (f)
Snack (morning)	Znüni (m)
Snack (afternoon)	Zvieri (m)

Food & Drinks

Meat Preparation

rare	bluetig
medium	medium
	halb durä
well done	guät durä

Key Measurements

Kilo	Kilo (n)
Litre	Liter (m)
Pound	Pfund (n)

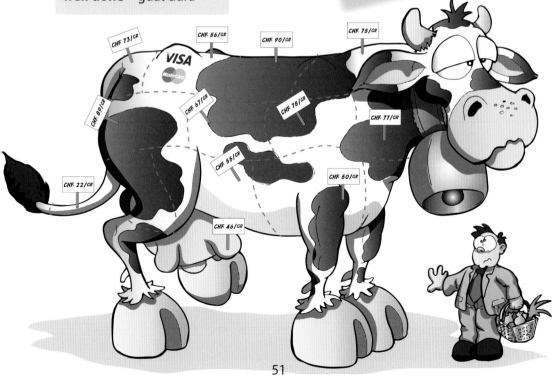

Food & Drinks

Coffee & Hot Drinks

Cappuccino	Cappuccino (m) *(Gaputschino)*	**Punch**	Punsch (m)
Coffee (with cream)	Kafi (crème) (m)	**Hot chocolate**	Haissi Schoggi (f)
Coffee with milk	Milchkafi (m) Schalä (f)	**Hot milk**	Haissi Milch (f)
		Latte Macchiato	Latte Macchiato (f) *(Latte Maggiato)*
Expresso	Espresso (m)	**Tea**	Tee (m)

BE AWARE... The Swiss tend to call **'Tee'** any type of water infusion, so if you want a cup of black tea with milk it is better to specify: **'Schwarztee mit crème'** or just **'Tee crème'.**

Cold Drinks

Cold drinks	Chalti Getränk (pl)
Apple juice	Öpfelsaft (m) Süässmoscht (m)
Coke	Coggi (n)/ Cola (n)
Grapefruit juice	Grapefruitsaft (m) *(Gräpfrüsaft)*
Grape juice	Truubesaft (m)
Iced tea	Iis-tee (m)
Juice	Saft (m)
Mineral water	Mineralwasser (n)
Orange juice	Orangschäsaft (m) / O-Saft (m)
Soft drink	Blööterliwasser (n)
Cold chocolate	Chalti Schoggi (f)
Water with gas	Wasser mit Cholesüüri / Blööterli
Water without gas	Wasser ooni Cholesüüri / Blööterli

Typical Swiss drinks

For children, **haissi Ovi / Ovo** (hot ovaltine).

In summer typical drinks are: **än Gsprüzztä** (white wine with water and lemon), **äs Panaché** (beer with lemonade) or a **Schtangä** (draft beer).

Typical winter drinks include: **Schümli Pflümli** (coffee with spirits and whipped cream), **Kafi Schnaps** (coffee with spirit), **Jägertee** (tea with spirit), **Punsch** (punch), or **Glüäwii** (hot wine).

In autumn you may find **Suser** (half fermented wine).

Alcohol	
Beer	Biär (n)
Cider	suurä Moscht (m)
Digestive	Vertailer (m)
	Digestive (m)
	(Dischestiv)
Draft beer	Schtangä (f)
Hot wine	Glüäwii (m)
Spirit	Schnaps (m)
Wine	Wii (m)
Red wine	Rotwii (m)
	Rotä (m)
White wine	Wiisswii (m)
	Wiissä (m)
A glass of Champagne	Güppli (n)

Food & Drinks

Food & Drinks

Seafood

Crab	Krabä (f)
Fish	Fisch (m)
Pike-perch	Zander (m)
Lobster	Hummer (m)
Perch	Egli (m)
	Barsch (m)
Pike	Hecht (m)
Prawns	Riisecrevettä (f)
	(Riisägröwettä)
Salmon	Lachs (m)
Seafood	Meeresfrücht (pl)
Shrimp	Crevettä (f) *(Gröwettä)*
Trout	Forälä (f)
Tuna	Ton (m)
White fish	Felchä (f)

Fruit

Apple	Öpfel (m)
Banana	Bananä (f)
Cherry	Chriäsi (n)
Fruit	Frucht (f)
Lemon	Zitrone (f)
Lime	Limone (f)
Tangerine	Mandarinli (n)
Orange	Orangschä (f)
Pear	Birä (f)
Raspberry	Himbeeri (n)
Strawberry	Erdbeeri (n)
Watermelon	Wassermelonä (f)

Flavours

Flavour	Gschmakk (m)
bitter	bitter
spicy	scharf
mild	mild
over salted	versalzä
salty	salzig
sour	suur
sweet	süäss
tasteless	fad
	gschmakklos

Vegetables & Legumes

Beans	Boonä (f)	Lettuce	Chopfsalat (m)
Broccoli	Broggoli (m)	Onion	Zwiblä (f)
Carrots	Rüäbli (n)		Bölä (pl)
Cauliflower	Bluämächöl (m)	Pepper	Pepperoni (f)
Eggplant	Oberschinä (f)	Potatoes	Herdöpfel (m)
Garlic	Chnobli (m)	Salad	Salat (m)
	Chnoblauch (m)	Spinach	Schpinat (m)
Lentils	Linsä (pl)	Tomato	Tomatä (f)
Legumes	Hülsäfrücht (pl)	Vegetables	Gmüäs (n)

Typical Swiss Dishes

Chäsfondue (*Chäsfondü*)	Melted Cheese dipped with bread
Raclette (*Ragglett*)	Melted Cheese, eaten with potatoes
Röschti	Potato tortilla
Zürigschnäzzläts	Sliced meat (e.g. veal) with a cream sauce
Birchermüesli	Muesli with fruit, oats and yoghurt
Vermicelles (*Wermisell*)	Dessert made of chestnuts

Food & Drinks

Other Food

Egg	Ai (n)	**Ice cream**	Glacé (n) (*Glasse*)
Butter	Butter (m)	**Jam**	Gomfi (f)
	Ankä (m)	**Margarine**	Margerinä (f)
Candy	Zältli (n)	**Marmalade**	Orangschägomfi (f)
Condiment	Aromat (n)	**Olive oil**	Olivenöl (n)
	Gwürz (pl)	**Pasta**	Pasta (f)
Corn	Mais (m)		Taigwarä (pl)
Corn on the cob	Mais-cholbä (m)	**Peanut butter**	Erdnussbutter (m)
Dressing	Salatsossä (f)	**Rice**	Riis (m)
Flour	Määl (n)	**Sugar**	Zukker (m)
Honey	Honig (m)	**Vinegar**	Essig (m)

Food & Drinks

Bread

Baguette	Pariserbrot (n)
Bread	Brot (n)
brown bread	dunkels Brot (n)
Cake	Chuächä (m)
Croissant	Gipfeli (n)
Jam doughnut	Berliner (m)
Pastry	Gebäkk (n)
Pie	Wäjä (f)
Roll	Brötli (n) / Pürli (n)
Sandwich	Sandwich (m) *(Sändwitsch)*
Toast	Tooscht (m)
White bread	Wiissbrot (n)
Whole grain bread	Vollkornbrot (n)

Preparations

fried	prötlet
boiled	gkocht
deep fried	frittiert
grilled	griliert
marinated	mariniert
raw	roo
roasted	gröschtet

Shopping

Groceries	Läbesmittel (pl)
Bakery	Bekk (m)
	Bekkerei (f)
Butcher's shop	Mezzg(erei) (f)
Deli (katessen)	Delikatessladä (m)
fresh	früsch
frozen	tüfgfrorä
Shop	Ladä (m)
shopping	iichauffä
Supermarket	Supermärt (m)
Fruits of the season	aktuelli Frücht
	säsonali Frücht

Dairy Products

Yoghurt	Joghurt (n) *(Jogurt)*
Cheese	Chäs (m)
Cream	Raam (m)
Curd cheese	Quark (m)
Milk	Milch (f)

 **TIP...** In Switzerland, it is common practice to share the bill if you are in a restaurant or bar with someone else. On such occasions, the waiter will usually ask you:

Zaled Sii trännt oder mitenand?
(Are you paying separately or together?)
The answer then is:
Trännt bitte (separate) or
Mitenand (together).

 TIP... It is also common for a waiter to ask, after a meal, whether the food was good **'Isch äs guät gsi?'** This is not merely a polite question, but an opportunity to bring in some feedback.

Diets

Diet	Diät (f)
diabetic	diabetisch
kosher	koscher
halal	halal
vegan	vegan(isch)
vegetarian	vegetarisch

Does the meal contain pork / meat?
Hätt's Schweineflaisch / Flaisch i däm Essä?
Do you have vegetarian dishes?
Händ Sii au Vegi-Menüs?

WOULD YOU LIKE ME TO SPLIT THE BILL?

Places to Eat

		Canteen	Kantinä (f)
Bar	Bar (f)		Mensa (f)
Restaurant	Reschtorant (n)	Take away	Take away (m)
	Baiz (f)		(Teik Awei)
Coffee bar/cafe	Kafi (n)	Dining car	Schpiiswagä (m)

57

Health

I NEED:
6 PACKETS OF CONDOMS
2 NICOTINE PATCHES
AND A PACKET OF ASPIRIN...

Health & Safety

Key Survival Phrases

I don't feel well.	Ich füül mich nöd wool.
I feel sick.	Mir isch schlächt.
	Ich füül mich chrank.
Where can I find a pharmacy?	Wo hätt's än Apothek?
I need something for...	Ich bruchä n'öppis gägä...
Do I need a prescription?	Bruch ich äs Rezäpt?
I am allergic to...	Ich bin allergisch gägä...
Do you have something for...?	Händ Sii öppis gägä...? (fr)
I need my glasses.	Ich bruchä mini Brülä.
I think I'm going to be sick.	Ich glaub, mir wird schlächt.
I have diarrhoea.	Ich ha Durchfall.
I need a pill.	Ich bruchä ä Tablettä.
I'm bleeding.	Ich blüätä.
That doesn't look very safe.	Das gseet nöd grad sicher us.
I have a headache / toothache.	Ich ha Chopfwee / Zaawee.

Key Survival Phrases	
He / she has a concussion.	Er / Sii hätt ä Ghirnerschütterig.
fall down / I fell down.	umfallä, umgheiä / Ich bin umgfallä.
	Ich bi gschtürzt.
I stumbled.	Ich bi gschtürchlet / gschtolperet.
I broke my arm / leg / foot.	Ich ha mir dä Arm / s'Bai / dä Fuäss brochä.
My stomach / head / tooth hurts.	Min Magä / Chopf / Zaa tuät wee.
Are you pregnant?	Sind Sii schwanger? (fr)
When was your last period?	Wänn händ Sii sletscht Mal Iri Täg ka? (fr)
Do you take any hormones?	Nämed Sii Hormon? (fr)
Do you take any medicine?	Nämed Sii Medikamänt? (fr)
Do you take drugs?	Nämed Sii Drogä? (fr)
Do you drink alcohol?	Trinked Sii Alkohol? (fr)
Do you smoke?	Rauched Sii? (fr)
Do you have a private insurance?	Sind Sii privat versicheret? (fr)
Do you have any hereditary illnesses in your family?	Händ Sii Erbchrankhaitä i dä Familiä? (fr)

ONCE AGAIN !...THIS IS NOT THE RED CROSS, AND THIS IS NOT A VACCINATION CENTRE ! THIS IS THE SWISS EMBASSY...

Health & Safety

ALL WHAT I DID WAS BRING HIM THE BILL...

BILL

Hospital

Ambulance	Ambulanz (f)	**Patient**	Paziänt (m)
	Chrankäwagä (m)		Paziäntin (f)
Clinic	Klinik (f)	**Prescription**	Rezäpt (n)
Doctor	Arzt (m) / Ärztin (f)	**Ward**	Schtazion(f)
Doctor's surgery	Praxis (f)		Abtailig (f)
Emergency	Notfall (m)	**Intensive care**	Intensivschtazion (f)
Hospital	Schpital (n)	**First Aid**	Erschti Hilf (f)
Emergency room	Notufnaam (f)	**Nurse ***	Chrankäschwöschter (f)

BE AWARE... * The name for nurse has recently changed from **'Chrankäschwöschter'** (Illness sister) to **'Pflägfachfrau / maa'** (Care specialist). The reason is that the profession has evolved and nurses in Switzerland didn't want to continue being associated with the nun community who were, originally, the ones doing this task.

60

Health Problems

Abscess	Apszäss (m)	**Fever**	Fiäber (n)
allergic to	alergisch gägä	**Flu**	Grippe (f)
Allergy	Alergii (f)	**Hay fever**	Hoischnuppä (m)
Appendicitis (f)	Blinddarmenzündig	**Headache**	Chopfwee (n)
		Infection	Enzündig (f)
Asthma	Aschtma (n)	**Injury**	Verlezzig (f)
Blood pressure	Bluätdrukk (m)	**Insomnia**	Schlaflosikait (f)
Blood sugar	Bluätzukker (m)	**Pain**	Schmärzä (pl)
Broken bone	Chnochäbruch (m)	**Parasite**	Parasit (m)
burn / burned	verbränä	**Poison**	Gift (n)
	verbrännt	**poisoned**	vergiftet
Cold	Vercheltig (f)	**Rabies**	Tollwuät (f)
Concussion	Ghirnerschütterig (f)	**sick**	chrank
contagious	aschtekkänd	**Stomach ache**	Buuchwee (n)
Cramp	Chrampf (m)	**Temperature**	Temperatur (f)
Diabetes	Diabetis (f)	**to cough**	huäschtä
Diarrhoea	Durchfall (m)	**Virus**	Wirus (m)

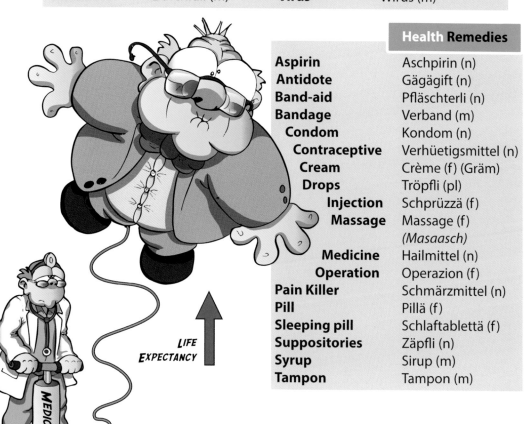

LIFE
EXPECTANCY

MEDICINE

Health Remedies

Aspirin	Aschpirin (n)
Antidote	Gägägift (n)
Band-aid	Pfläschterli (n)
Bandage	Verband (m)
Condom	Kondom (n)
Contraceptive	Verhüetigsmittel (n)
Cream	Crème (f) (Gräm)
Drops	Tröpfli (pl)
Injection	Schprüzzä (f)
Massage	Massage (f) (Masaasch)
Medicine	Hailmittel (n)
Operation	Operazion (f)
Pain Killer	Schmärzmittel (n)
Pill	Pillä (f)
Sleeping pill	Schlaftablettä (f)
Suppositories	Zäpfli (n)
Syrup	Sirup (m)
Tampon	Tampon (m)

Health & Safety

Human Body

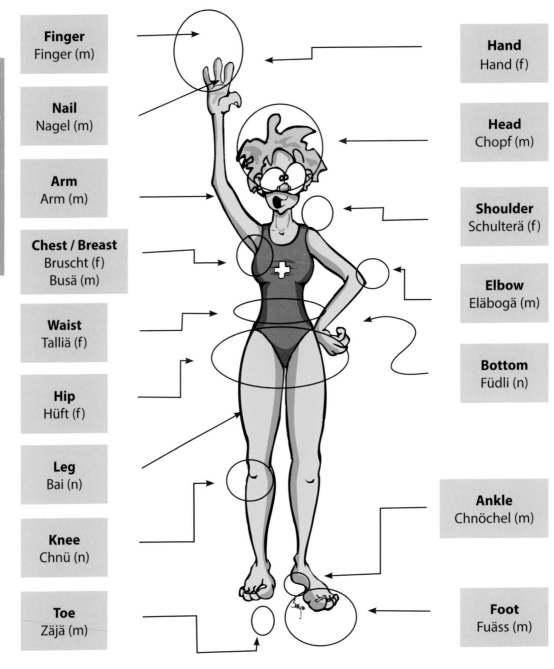

Finger
Finger (m)

Nail
Nagel (m)

Arm
Arm (m)

Chest / Breast
Bruscht (f)
Busä (m)

Waist
Talliä (f)

Hip
Hüft (f)

Leg
Bai (n)

Knee
Chnü (n)

Toe
Zäjä (m)

Hand
Hand (f)

Head
Chopf (m)

Shoulder
Schulterä (f)

Elbow
Eläbogä (m)

Bottom
Füdli (n)

Ankle
Chnöchel (m)

Foot
Fuäss (m)

Health & Safety

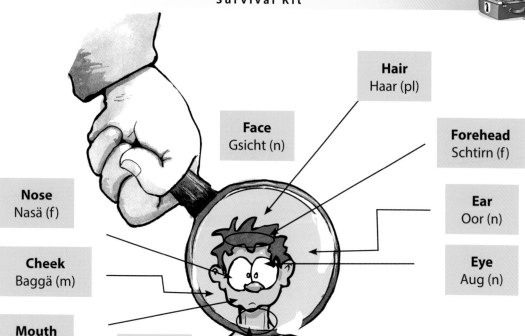

Hair
Haar (pl)

Face
Gsicht (n)

Forehead
Schtirn (f)

Nose
Nasä (f)

Ear
Oor (n)

Cheek
Baggä (m)

Eye
Aug (n)

Mouth
Muul (n)

Throat
Hals (m)

Health & Safety

Other Body Parts

Eyebrow	Augebrauä (f)
Eyelash	Wimperä (pl)
Fingernail	Fingernagel (m)
Blood	Bluät (n)
Heart	Härz (n)
Skin	Huut (f)
Penis	Penis (m)
Back	Ruggä (m)
Neck	Nakkä (f)
Toenail	Zäjänagel (m)
Freckles	Märzetüpfli (pl)
	Summerschprossä (pl)
Tooth	Zaa (m)
Tongue	Zungä (f)
Vagina	Vagina (f)

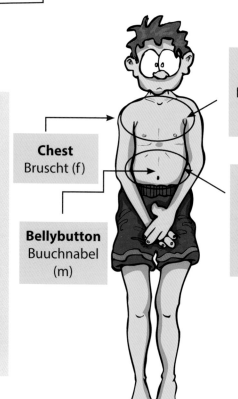

Nipple
Bruschtwarzä (f)

Chest
Bruscht (f)

Abdomen
Buuch (m)

Bellybutton
Buuchnabel (m)

Stomach
Magä (m)

BE AWARE... In High German smell is **'riechen'** and taste is **'schmecken'**. Swiss German, on the other hand, doesn't distinguish between the two, and uses the verb **'schmökkä'** for both.

Health & Safety

Body Activities

Eyes:

blink	blinzlä
cry	brüälä
	hüüla
wink	zwinkerä
stare	schtarrä
look / watch	luägä
see	gsee
I am short-sighted.	Ich bi churzsichtig.
I am long-sighted.	Ich bi wiitsichtig.

Ears:

listen	losä
hear	ghörä
wiggle	gwagglä (mit dä Oorä gwagglä)

Mouth:

smile	lächlä
laugh	lachä
whisper	flüschterä
kiss	küssä
lick	lutschä
suck	sugä
speak	redä
yawn	gäänä
cough	huäschtä
burp	görpsä
	babys: görpslä

Hands:

touch	berüärä
	aalangä
press	drukkä
hug	umarmä
shake	schüttlä
fold	faltä
pray	bätä
hold	hebä
grab	griiffä
	feschthebä

Nose:

smell	schmökkä
blow one's nose	sich d'Nasä puzzä
cover	zuähebä

Skin:

blush	root werdä
get wrinkles	Faltä übercho
dry out	uuströchnä
Goose bumps	Huänerhuut (f)
to get goose bumps	Huänärhuut übercho
to break out in a rash	än Uus-schlag übercho

Emotions

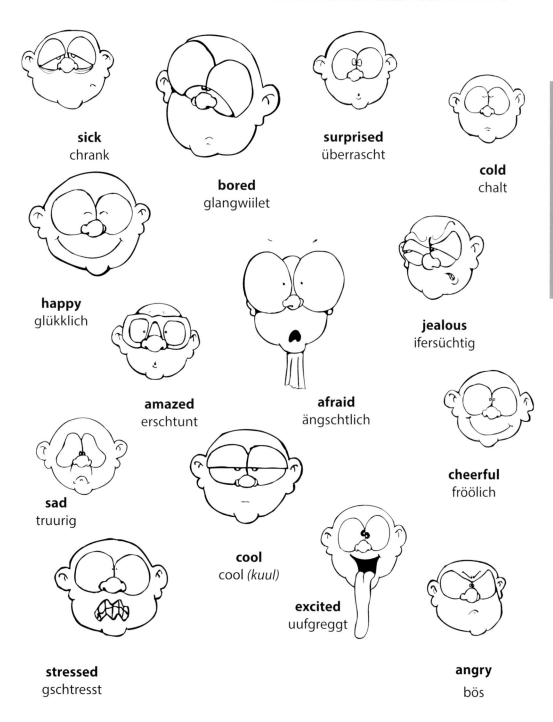

sick
chrank

bored
glangwiilet

surprised
überrascht

cold
chalt

happy
glükklich

jealous
ifersüchtig

amazed
erschtunt

afraid
ängschtlich

sad
truurig

cheerful
fröölich

cool
cool *(kuul)*

excited
uufgreggt

stressed
gschtresst

angry
bös

Health & Safety

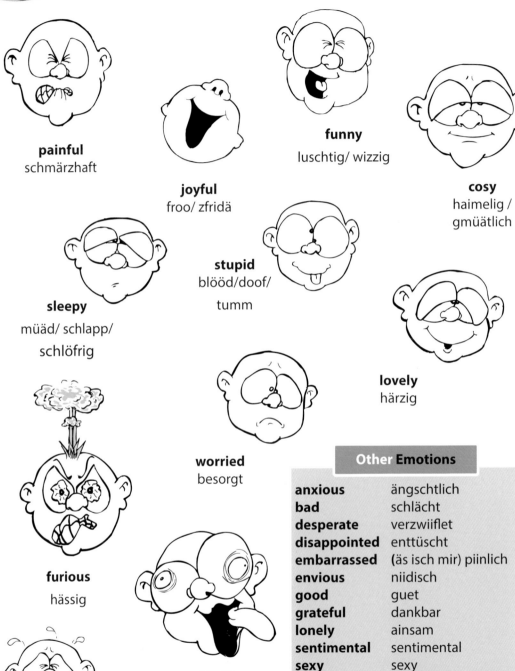

painful
schmärzhaft

joyful
froo/ zfridä

funny
luschtig/ wizzig

cosy
haimelig /
gmüätlich

sleepy
müäd/ schlapp/
schlöfrig

stupid
blööd/doof/
tumm

lovely
härzig

worried
besorgt

furious
hässig

crazy
verrukkt/ gaga/ irr

depressed
depressiv

Other Emotions	
anxious	ängschtlich
bad	schlächt
desperate	verzwiiflet
disappointed	enttüscht
embarrassed	(äs isch mir) piinlich
envious	niidisch
good	guet
grateful	dankbar
lonely	ainsam
sentimental	sentimental
sexy	sexy
shy	schüch
so-so	so so (la la)
vigorous	energisch
horny	schpizz
	giggerig

Swiss Expressions

Deciphering Swiss expressions may be a challenge; therefore, the following illustrations can be used as a guideline:

 = **HAPPY**
glükklich

 = **SAD**
truurig

 = **ANGRY**
bös

 = **COOL**
cool
(kuul)

 = **CRAZY**
verrukkt/ gaga/
irr

Emergency

Emergencies

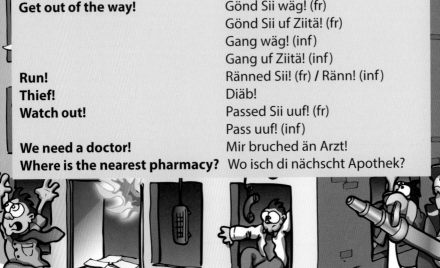

Fire Dept.	Fürweer (f)
Police	Polizai (f)
Emergency	Notfall (m)
An avalanche!	Ä Lawinä!
Be careful!	Achtung!
Call an ambulance!	Ruäfed Sii än Chrankäwagä! (fr)
	Rüäf än Chrankäwagä! (inf)
Call the police!	Lütet Sii dä Polizai a! (fr)
	Lüt dä Polizai a! (inf)
Can someone call a doctor?	Chann öpper amenä Arzt aalütä?
Someone is following me!	Öpper verfolgt mich!
Fire!	Füür!
Help!	Hilfe (f)!
Hurry!	Schnäll!
Jump!	Gump!
I am a diabetic.	Ich bi Diabetiker / in.
She is pregnant.	Sii isch schwanger.
I am pregnant.	Ich bi schwanger.
Is there a doctor?	Isch än Arzt da?
It's an emergency!	Äs isch än Notfall!
Get out of the way!	Gönd Sii wäg! (fr)
	Gönd Sii uf Ziitä! (fr)
	Gang wäg! (inf)
	Gang uf Ziitä! (inf)
Run!	Ränned Sii! (fr) / Ränn! (inf)
Thief!	Diäb!
Watch out!	Passed Sii uuf! (fr)
	Pass uuf! (inf)
We need a doctor!	Mir bruched än Arzt!
Where is the nearest pharmacy?	Wo isch di nächscht Apothek?

Health & Safety

Police

Police

Someone stole my wallet.	Mis Portmonee isch gschtolä wordä.
I want to report a stolen…	Ich möcht mis gschtolne… meldä.
You should go to the police.	Sii söttet zu dä Polizai gaa. (fr)
	Du söttsch zu dä Polizai gaa. (inf)
Can you please call the police?	Chönd Sii bitte dä Polizai aalütä? (fr)
I've been robbed!	Ich bi beschtolä wordä!
I saw what happened.	I ha gsee, was passiert isch.
What's the fine for?	Für was isch diä Puäss?
How much is the fine?	Wiä vill choschtet diä Puäss?
Where is the police station?	Wo isch dä nächscht Polizaiposchtä?

Health & Safety

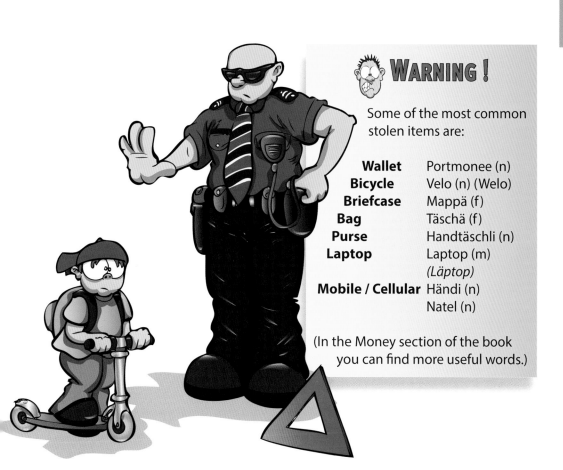

WARNING !

Some of the most common stolen items are:

Wallet	Portmonee (n)
Bicycle	Velo (n) (Welo)
Briefcase	Mappä (f)
Bag	Täschä (f)
Purse	Handtäschli (n)
Laptop	Laptop (m) *(Läptop)*
Mobile / Cellular	Händi (n)
	Natel (n)

(In the Money section of the book you can find more useful words.)

Health & Safety

Immigration & Customs

Permit	Bewilligung (f)
	Genemigung (f)
Visa	Wisum (n)
Foreigner	Ussländer/in (m/f)
Customs	Zoll (m)
Frontier / Border	Gränzä (f)
to declare (at customs)	verzollä
to immigrate	iiraisä
to emigrate	uusraisä
a valid visa	äs gültigs Wisum
renew a visa	äs Wisum verlängerä
Residence permit	Ufenthaltsgenemigung (f)
to apply for a visa	äs Wisum beaträgä
What kind of a visa do you have?	Was für äs Wisum händ Sii? (fr)
I want to work in Switzerland.	Ich möcht i dä Schwiiz schaffä.
How can I apply for a visa?	Wiä chann ich äs Wisum beaträgä?
I have something to declare.	Ich ha öppis z'verzollä.
I have nothing to declare.	Ich ha nüt z'verzollä.
Do you have anything to declare?	Händ Sii öppis z'verzollä? (fr)
I want to stay in Switzerland for 3 months.	Ich möcht drü Mönät i dä Schwiiz bliibä.
I am married to a Swiss.	Ich bi mit ämä Schwiizer ghüratä (with a Swiss man).
	Ich bi mit ärä Schwiizerin ghüratä (with a Swiss woman).

The most common permits for foreigners in Switzerland are:

1. C-Permit (C-Bewilligung), Niderlassigsbewilligung: unlimited residency in Switzerland.

2. B-Permit (B-Bewilligung), Jaaresbewilligung: usually has to be renewed each year.

3. L-Permit (L-Bewilligung) : Short-term Work or Residence Permit.

4. G-Permit Gränzgänger-Bewilligung: border crosser permit.

5. Turischtäwisum (Tourist Visa): usually valid for three months.

Shopping in General

...BUT FOR EVERY 100 GMS.

OFFER 1.⁵⁰

TIP... The Basic Five...

Open
Closed
offä (adj.),
uufmachä (verb)
zuä (adj.)
zuämachä (verb)

Entrance
Exit
Emergency Exit
ligang (m)
Usgang (m)
Notusgang (m)

BE AWARE... The biggest retailers in Switzerland own not only supermarkets, but also a vast variety of other types of shops. As they all have the same 'customer incentive' strategies, it is most likely that some shops will ask you before you pay if you have their shopping card (**Händ Sii ä ...Chartä?**), which allows customers to collect bonus points for every purchase.

Key Survival Words

Bookshop	Buächhandlig (f)	**On sale**	Uusverchauff
	Büächerladä (m)	**Price**	Priis (m)
Brand	Markä (f)	**Security**	Sicherhait (f)
Cashier	Kassierer (m)	**Shopping bag**	lichaufs-Täschä (f)
	Kassiererin (f)	**Store**	Ladä (m)
complain	sich beklagä /chlönä	**Shopping centre**	Ichaufszentrum (n)
	mozzä	**to buy**	poschtä, chauffä
Department	Abtailig (f)	**to order**	pschtelä
Discount	reduziert	**to sell**	verchauffä
Electrical shop	Elektrogschäft (n)		

72

Key Survival Shopping Phrases

to go shopping	lädälä
Do you have…?	Händ Sii…? (fr)
I'm looking for…	Ich suächä…
How much does it cost?	Wiä vill choschtet das?
How much does this cost?	Wiä vill choschtet das? Wiä tüür isch das?
At what time do you open?	Wänn mached Sii uuf?
At what time do you close?	Wänn mached Sii zuä?
	Ab wänn händ Sii zuä?
Do you have something cheaper?	Git's au öppis Günschtigers?
That's expensive!	Das isch tüür!
Can you give me…?	Chönd Sii mir … gä? (fr)
Do you accept credit cards?	Nämed Sii Kreditchartä? (fr)
I need a shopping bag.	Ich bruchä än Plastiksakk / ä Tragtäschä.
I would like to try it on.	Chann ich das mal probierä?
How long is the warranty / guarantee?	Wiä lang gits Garantii?
I want my money back!	Ich will mis Gäld zrugg!
I will take this.	Ich nimm das.
I'm just browsing.	Ich luägä nu echli.
Where is the exit?	Wo isch dä Notusgang?
Do you have a larger / smaller size?	Händ Sii das au grösser? chlinner?(fr)
Can you please give me a receipt?	Chönd Sii mir ä Quittig gee? (fr)

Shopping

A 'BASELDÜTSCH' DICTIONARY…?
YES SIR, UPSTAIRS, IN THE CROSSWORDS
AND PUZZLES SECTION…

Clothes

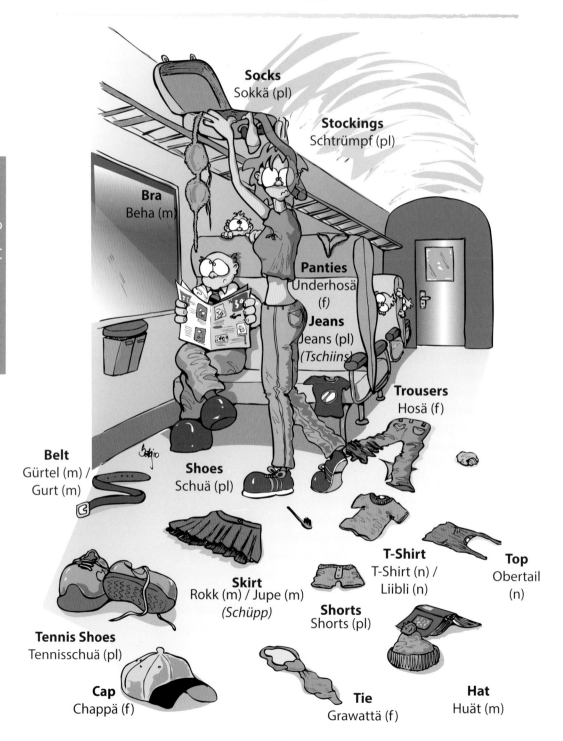

Socks
Sokkä (pl)

Stockings
Schtrümpf (pl)

Bra
Beha (m)

Panties
Underhosä (f)

Jeans
Jeans (pl)
(Tschiins)

Trousers
Hosä (f)

Belt
Gürtel (m) /
Gurt (m)

Shoes
Schuä (pl)

T-Shirt
T-Shirt (n) /
Liibli (n)

Top
Obertail
(n)

Skirt
Rokk (m) / Jupe (m)
(Schüpp)

Shorts
Shorts (pl)

Tennis Shoes
Tennisschuä (pl)

Cap
Chappä (f)

Tie
Grawattä (f)

Hat
Huät (m)

74

Clothes & Accessories

Blouse	Blusä (f)	**Evening dress**	Aabigchlaid (n)
Button	Chnopf (m)	**Gloves**	Häntschä (pl)
Clothing	Chlaider (pl)	**Jacket**	Jagge (f)
Coat	Mantel (m)	**Scarf**	Schal (m) / Tuäch (n)
Collar	Chragä (m)	**Shirt**	Hämp (n)
Suit	Koschtüm (n)	**short sleeves**	churzärmlig
Dress (noun)	Chlaid (n)	**long sleeves**	langärmlig
dress (verb)	aaziiä	**Underwear**	Underwösch (f)
dressed	aazogä	**Wallet**	Portmonee (n)

Clothing Materials

The following is a list of the most common textiles:

Cotton	Baumwule (f)
Leather	Läder (n)
Linen	Liinä (f)
Nylon	Nylon (n) (Nailon)
Polyester	Polyester (m) (Polijeschter)
Silk	Sidä (f)
Wool	Wulä (f)

Shopping

75

Money & banking

SWISS BANK

...THE DOLLAR KEEPS DROPPING, THE STERLING IS UNSTABLE, AND WHO KNOWS WHERE THE EURO IS HEADING...IN OTHER WORDS, WE'RE BACK IN BUSINESS!

Shopping

Money

Money	Gäld (n)
Bank	Bank (f)
Bank account	Bankkonto (n)
Banknotes	Banknotä (f)
Cash	Cash (n) (Käsch)
	Bargäld (n)
Cash machine	Gäldautomat (m)
Cheque	Schegg (m)
Coin	Münzä (f)
Counter	Schalter (m)
Credit card	Kreditchartä (f)
Currency	Wäärig (f)
Debit card	EC-Chartä (f) (Eze-Chartä)
	Poschtchartä (f)
Deposit	Depot (n) *(Depo)*
	Hinderlegig (f)
earn money	Gäld verdiänä
Exchange rate	Wächselratä (f)
Income	Iikomä (n)
Interest	Zins (m)
invest money	Gäld inweschtierä
Investment	Inweschtizion (f)
	Inweschtierig (f)
Loan	Darleä (n)
Loss	Verluscht (m)
Payment	Zalig (f)
Profit	Profit (m)
Rappen *	Rappä (m)
Savings account	Schparkonto (n)
Signature	Unterschrift (f)
Small change	Münz (n)
Swiss franc	Schwiizer Frankä (m)
to pay	zalä
to save	schparä
to spend	uusgä
to transfer	überwiisä
Travellers' cheques	Traveller cheques (pl) (Träwälär Schegg)
to withdraw	abhebä

* 100 Rappen = 1 Swiss Franc

Money, Banks and Exchange Office

What's the exchange rate today for British pounds / dollars?
Wiä isch dä Wächselkurs für Britischi Pfund / Dollar hüt?

Can you please change this banknote for small change?
Chönd Sii mir das Nötli wechslä? (fr)

Do you have change for this?
Chönd Sii mir das i Münz wächslä? (fr)

I don't have any money.
Ich ha kai Gäld.

Your cash machine kept my card!
Dä Gäldautomat hätt mini Chartä iäzogä!

How many francs do I get for X dollars?
Wiä vill frankä chumm ich für X Dollar über?

I would like to open a bank account / savings account.
Ich möcht äs Bankkonto/ Schparkonto erröffnä.

to put money aside
Gäld schparä / Gäld uf Ziitä legä / Gäld uf di höch
Kantä legä

Shopping

Transportation

ZVV S-Bahnen, Busse und Schiffe
S-Bahn trains, buses and boats

ZVV Survival Phrases

Where is the tram/bus timetable? Wo isch dä Tram-/Bus-Faarplan?

Where is the next tram/bus stop? Wo isch diä nächscht Tram-/Bus-haltschtell?

Would you like to sit down? Möchted Sii sizzä/absizzä? (fr)

May I sit down? Chann ich bitte sizzä/absizzä/anäsizzä?

What's the name of this stop? Wiä haisst diä Haltschtell?

Does this tram go to ....? Gaat/Faart das Tram uf/an…?

Which tram takes me to …..? Welläs Tram faart/gaat uf/an…?

Do you need help? Chann ich Innä hälfä? Bruched Sii Hilf? (fr)

Could you please hold the door open for me? Chönd Sii mir bitte trukkä? (fr)

Could you please help me with my stroller/bags? Chönd Sii mir bitte mit äm Koffer/Gepäkk hälfä?(fr)

Can you help me get a ticket from the ticket machine please?
Chönd Sii mir hälfä äs Billet z'lösä? (fr)

Excuse me, your bicycle is on top of my dog.
Äxgüsi, Iräs Welo isch uf mim Hund obä. (fr)

How to use the ZVV tram/bus ticket machines in Zurich

short-distance tickets (up to 4 stops) touch here to see the valid stops

Other connections. Zone upgrades.

Zone 110 (only Zurich) only for 1 hour

Multiple tickets (multiple-journey tickets, multiple day passes etc.)

Zone 110 (only Zurich) for 24 hours

for people purchasing tickets after 9 in the morning (cheaper!)

To the Zurich Airport

The ZurichCARD offers unlimited transport, for limited time in and around the city of Zurich, plus great touristic deals.

To Winterthur

Free choice of alternative departure locations

Touch here for text in **English**

BE AWARE... Tickets have to be bought before departure. There is no possibility to buy tickets on trains, buses and trams.

Travelling

Key Survival Phrases

I have lost my ticket.	Ich ha mis Bilet verlorä.
I bought the wrong ticket.	Ich ha s`falsch Bilet kauft.
Does this train / bus stop at…?	Haltet dä Zug / Bus bi.. / in..?
When does the next train for…leave?	Wänn faart dä nächschti Zug uf…?
Is this the train / bus to….?	Isch das dä Zug / Bus uf…?
At what time does the train from…arrive?	Wänn chunnt dä Zug vo…aa?
On what platform does the next train for… leave?	Uf welläm Glais faart dä Zug uf…?

WARNING !

What Ticket Controllers Will Usually Ask...

Ali Bilet bitte!
All tickets please (request to show tickets).

Wohär chömed Sii? / Wo sind Sii iigstigä?
Where are you coming from?

Wo anä faared Sii?
Where are you going?

Händ Sii äs gültigs Bilet?
Do you have a valid ticket?

ALLI BILET BITTE

Translation: Tickets please.

TIP… There are different tickets with special price offers to travel around Switzerland. The main offers are:

GA (n) (Generalabonnement): an unlimited ticket valid for most of public transport in Switzerland.

Halbtax (n): a card that allows you to buy tickets for most public transport at half price.

Tages-chartä (f): a 'one-day ticket' valid for most of public transport in Switzerland.

Familiä-chartä (f): a ticket for families, which offers reduced prices for children.

Website: **www.sbb.ch/en**

BE AWARE… All public announcements over the loudspeakers are made in High-German. Only on very rare occasions is Swiss German used.

Key Survival Phrases

A ticket to..., please.	Äs Bilet uf ..., bitte.
How much does a ticket to...cost?	Wiä vill choschtet s'Bilet uf...?
Window / aisle	Am Fänschter / bim Gang
No smoking	Nichtraucher
single / one way ticket	nur hii / aifach
Return ticket	hii und zrugg / hii und retour *(rötur)*
Do I have to change trains?	Muäs ich umschtigä?
Where do I have to change...?	Wo muäs ich umschtiigä?
The train / bus is delayed.	Dä Zug / Bus hätt Verschpötig.
on foot	z`Fuäss
by car / by bike	mit äm Auto / Velo
by plane / by train	mit äm Flugzüg / mit äm Zug
The flight is cancelled.	Dä Flug isch anuliert.
Where can I get a taxi?	Wo hätt's äs Taxi?

Travel Words

Aeroplane	Flugzüg (n)	to reserve	reservierä
Arrival	Akunft (f)	Tourist	Turischt (m)
Bus	Bus (m)		Turischtin (f)
Bus stop	Bushalteschtell (f)	Train	Zug (m)
Bus ticket	Busbilet (n)	Train ticket	Zugbilet (n)
Car	Auto (n)	Train station	Baanhof (m)
City map	Schtadtplan (m)	Bus station	Busbaanhof (m)
Delay	Verschpötig (f)	Track	Glais (n)
Departure	Abrais (f)	Platform	Perron (n)
Driver's licence	Faaruuswis (m)	Petrol station	Tankschtell (f)
	Bilet (n)	Service area	Raschtplazz (m)
Plane ticket	Flugzüg-Tikket (n)		Raschtschtettä (f)
Highway/Motorway	Autobaan (f)	Speed camera	Radar (m)
Luggage	Gepäkk (n)	drive too fast	rasä
Passenger	Passagier (m)	leave	abfaarä
	(Passaschier)	land	landä
Passport	Pass (m)	to get on a bus	In Bus iischtigä
Petrol	Bänzin (n)	to get off a bus	Us äm Bus uusschtigä
Rucksack	Rukksakk (m)	Speed limit	Gschwindigkaits-
Space	Ruum (m)		begränzig (f)

Travelling

Directions

Travelling

Key Survival Phrases

to the left	nach linggs
to the right	nach rächts
around (the corner)	um (dä Eggä)
across (the bridge, the crossover)	über (d'Brugg, d'Überfüerig)
(X) streets from here	(X) Schtrassä wiitär
I'm looking for…	Ich suächä…
I think I am lost.	Ich glaub, ich ha mich verloffä.
Where? / in which direction?	wo? / i wellerä Richtig?
Do you know where… is?	Wüssed Sii, wo … isch? (fr)
	Waisch du, wo … isch? (inf)
Could you tell me the way to ….?	Chönted Sii mir sägä, wo ….isch? (fr)
How far is it to walk / to drive?	Wiä wiit isch äs zum Lauffä / zum Faarä?
Go straight on as far as the church.	Gönd Sii graduus bis zu dä Chilä. (fr)
Go along by the river.	Lauffed Sii am Fluss entlang. (fr)
along the street	dä Schtrass entlang

Continued on the next page….

Key Survival Phrases

Go up! / Go down!	Gönd Sii ufä! (fr)
	Gönd Sii abä! (fr)
up the stairs	d'Schtägä ufä
down the escalator	d'Rollträppä abä
go across the street	Gönd Sii über d'Schtrass. (fr)
Is it far / close?	Isch äs wiit / nöch?
behind the house	hinder s'Huus
in front of the house	vor s'Huus
through the market	dur dä Märt
to the station / to the church	bis zum Baanhof / zu dä Chilä
passing the school	a dä Schuäl verbii
leaving the village	us äm Dorf usä
entering the village	is Dorf inä
not far at all	nur än Chazzäschprung * / nöd wiit

only a stone's throw

Key Words

up	ufä
down	abä
left	linggs
right	rächts
here	da
there	deet
straight on	graduus
Map	Chartä (f)
	Schtadtplan (f)

Some Reference Points

Bridge	Brugg (f)
Cathedral	Katedraale (f)
Church	Chilä (f)
Corner	Eggä (m)
Crossing	Chrüüzig (f)
Mosque	Moschee (f)
School	Schuäl (f)
Street	Schtrass (f)
Synagogue	Synagogä (f)
Traffic light	Amplä (f)

Travelling

Travelling

Prepositions

TIP... When it comes to directions, prepositions are the most useful words to provide accurate information. This list shows the most common prepositions in Swiss German.

Key Prepositions

from	us	without	ooni
with / by (transport)	mit	until / by	bis
from / of	vo	at / on (vertical surfaces)	a(m)
at / by	bi	on (horizontal surfaces)	uf
after / according to	nach	behind	hinder
to	zu	in / into	in
across from / opposite	gägänüber	beside / next to	näbäd
		over / above / across	über
through	dur(ch)	under / beneath	under
against / into	gägä	in front of	vor
around	um	between	zwüschä
for	für	along	entlang

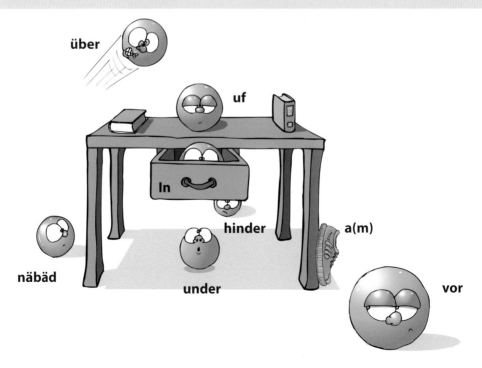

Hotel

...AND HOW DO YOU PREFER TO PAY, SIR: CASH, CREDIT CARD OR MORTGAGE..?

HOTEL

RECEPTION

Key Survival Phrases

Do you have a room?	Händ Sii no Zimmer frei? (fr)
Single / Double room please.	Äs Ainzelzimmer / äs Doppelzimmer, bitte.
Is breakfast included?	Isch dä Zmorgä im Priis inbegriffä?
with a view of the lake.	mit Seesicht
Can I have a morning call?	Chönd Sii mich telefonisch wekkä?
I want to check out.	Ich möcht uus-tschäggä.
Can I have the key to the room?	Dä Schlüssel fürs Zimmer...,bitte.
How much is it a night?	Wiä vill choschtets pro Nacht?
I will stay for.....nights.	Ich bliibe für .... Nächt.
I'd like to book...	Ich möcht... buächä.
I reserved a room in the name of....	Ich hann äs Zimmer für ... reserviert.
At what time is breakfast served?	Wänn chammär Zmorgä ässä?
a quiet room	äs ruigs Zimmer
a room with bath / with bath nearby	äs Zimmer mit Bad
	mit Etageduschi (*Etascheduschi*)
Youth hostel	Jugendhärbärg (f)

Hotel Words

B&B	B&B (n) *(Bi än Bi)*	**Wake up call**	Wekkaaruäf (m)
Bed	Bett (n)	**Pillow**	Chüssi (n)
Bed cover	Bettaazug (m)	**Reception**	Rezepzion (f)
Check in	iitschäggä	**Room**	Zimmer (n)
Check out	uus-tschäggä	**Room service**	Zimmerservice (m)
Concierge	Consierge (m)		*(Zimmer-Serwis)*
	(Gonsiersch)	**Slippers**	Finkä (pl)
Double bed	Doppelbett (n)	**Swimming pool**	Schwümmbad (n)
Gym	Fitnessruum (m)	**Towel**	Tüächli (n)
Key	Schlüssel (m)	**Full board**	Vollpension (f)
Lift	Lift (m)	**Half board**	Halbpension (f)
Lobby	Lobbi (f)		

Travelling

Outdoors

Geography

City	Schtadt(f)	**Park**	Park (m)
	City (f) *(Sitti)*	**Path**	Wäg (m)
Continent	Kontinänt (m)	**Peak**	Gipfel (m)
Country	Land (n)	**River**	Fluss (m)
Field	Fäld (n)	**Sea**	Meer (n)
Forest	Wald (m)	**State**	Schtaat (m)
Geography	Geografii (f)	**County**	Kanton (m)
Hill	Hügel (m)	**Town**	Schtadt (f)
Island	Inslä (f)	**Valley**	Taal (n)
Lake	See (m)	**Village**	Dörfli (n)
Mountain	Bärg (m)	**World**	Wält (f)
Ocean	Ozean (m)		

Travelling

Outdoor Snow Terms

Skiing	schiifaarä	**pretty girl skiing**	Schneehäsli (n)
I like skiing.	Ich faarä gärn	**Snowboard**	snöbä
	Schii.		bordä
Ski lift	Schiilift (m)		Snowboard faarä
Chair lift	Sässelilift (m)		*(Snoubord)*
easy hill to ski	Idiotähügel (m)	**Equipment**	Uusrüschtig (f)
Ski	Schii (m)	**Snow shoeing**	Schneeschuä lauffä
Ski boot	Schiischuä (m)	**Cross country skiing**	langloifflä
Ski school	Schiischuäl (f)	**Ski tour**	Schiiturä machä
Ski instructor	Schiileerer (m)	**Ski poles**	Schtökk (pl)
	Schiileererin (f)		

Other Snow Terms & Phrases

Partying and drinking after skiing	Après-ski (n) *(Aprä-Schii)*
Are you a good snowboarder?	Chasch du guät snowboard faarä? (inf)
I am a snowboarder.	Ich bin än Snöbär.
off the marked slope	ab dä Pischtä

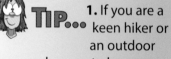

TIP... **1.** If you are a keen hiker or an outdoor person, be sure to become a member of **Rega (Swiss air rescue).** *

2. Hiking trails (**Wanderwäg**) in Switzerland are always marked with a yellow rhombus.

* website: **www.rega.ch/en**

Outdoor Mountain Terms

hike	wanderä
Hiking shoes	Wanderschuä (pl)
Grill area	Füürschtell (f)
Elevation gain	Höäunderschiid (m)
Provisions	Proviant (m)
Direction sign	Wägwiiser (m)
Swiss army knife	Sakkmässer (n)
Hiking path	Wanderwäg (m)
Picnic	Picnic (n) *(Piknik)*
Bicycle	Velo (n) *(Welo)*
camping	Camping (n) *(Kämping)*
walking	lauffä
driving	Auto faarä
paragliding	Glaitschirm flügä

Other Mountain Terms & Phrases

Is it steep?	Isch äs schtail?
How long do we have to climb?	Wiä lang müämmär ufelauffä?
How far away is the restaurant?	Wiä wiit isch äs no bis zu dä Baiz?

Travelling

Entertainment

Key Survival Phrases

What are your hobbies?	Was sind Iri Hobis? (fr)
	Was sind dini Hobis? (inf)
What do you do in your spare time?	Was mached Sii i Irerä Freiziit? (fr)
	Was machsch i dinerä Freiziit? (inf)
What do you like to do the most?	Was mached Sii am liäbschtä? (fr)
	Was machsch am liäbschtä? (inf)
I like cooking / eating / travelling.	Ich chochä / ässä / raisä gärn.
What's your favourite food?	Was isch dis Liäblingsässä? (inf)
I collect stamps.	Ich sammlä Briäfmarkä.
I like listening to music / watching TV.	Ich losä gärn Musig / Ich luäg gärn Fernse.
I read novels/ cartoons / the newspaper.	Ich läsä Romän / Comics / d'Ziitig.
I listen to classical music.	Ich losä klassischi Musig.
I jog regularly.	Ich tschoggä regelmässig.
I go (twice a week) to the gym.	Ich gang (zwaimal pro Wuchä) is Fitness.
I like playing golf / the piano / the violin.	Ich schpilä gärn Golf / Klavir / Giigä.

> **TIP...** For preferences, most Swiss use the adverb **'gärn'**, which is always placed after the verb: **Ich ässä gärn Bananä** (I like eating bananas).

Travelling

> **TIP...** Frequency is expressed with **'mal'**: **eimal** (once), **zwaimal** (twice), **drümal, viermal** etc. **'Pro'** means per, **pro Wuchä** (per week), **pro Monät** (per month) etc.

Key Survival Words

Book	Buäch (n)	**Library**	Bibliothek (f)
Concert	Konzärt (n)	**Humour**	Humoor (m)
to collect (cars)	(Auto) sammlä	**Joke**	Wizz (m)
dancing	tanzä	**Magic**	Zauberai (f)
dating	deitä		zaubärä (Verb)
Entertainment	Unterhaltig (f)	**Museum**	Museum (n)
Event	Event (m) *(iwent)*	**Music**	Musig (f)
	Aalass (m)	**Opera**	Operä (f)
Exhibition	Uus-schtellig (f)	**Party**	Party (f) *(Parti)*
to fish	fischä		Fäscht (n)
	anglä	**to play**	schpilä /geimä
Fitness	Fitness	**to play football**	tschutä
Beach	Schtrand (m)	**to read**	läsä
Cinema	Kino (n)	**to swim**	schwümä
Discotheque	Disco (f)	**Theatre**	Theater (n)
to gamble	schpilä / gämblä	**Wind surfing**	Wind sörfä
Game	Schpiil (n)	**Zoo**	Zoo (m)

Swiss Traditions

Carnival	Fasnacht (f)
blowing the alpenhorn	Alp-horn blasä
swinging flags	Faanäschwingä
Crossbow (shooting)	Armbruscht *(schüssä)*
milking	mälchä
Wood carving	schnizzä
yodelling	jodlä
Swiss wrestling	schwingä
throwing stones	Schtai stossä
swinging coins	Taler schwingä
Swiss accordion	Handörgeli (n)
making cheese	chäsä
Swiss traditional music	Ländler (m)

TIP... **Liäblings** means favourite and can be combined with lots of other words: **Liäblings-ässä** (favourite food), **Liäblings-film** (favourite movie), **Liäblings-reschtorant** (favourite restaurant).

Travelling

Family

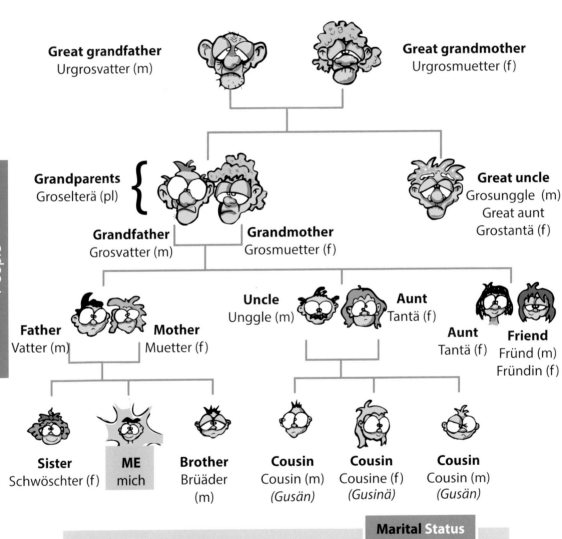

Family Tree

Great grandfather
Urgrosvatter (m)

Great grandmother
Urgrosmuetter (f)

Grandparents
Groselterä (pl)

Great uncle
Grosunggle (m)
Great aunt
Grostantä (f)

Grandfather
Grosvatter (m)

Grandmother
Grosmuetter (f)

Uncle
Unggle (m)

Aunt
Tantä (f)

Aunt
Tantä (f)

Friend
Fründ (m)
Fründin (f)

Father
Vatter (m)

Mother
Muetter (f)

People

Sister
Schwöschter (f)

ME
mich

Brother
Brüäder
(m)

Cousin
Cousin (m)
(Gusän)

Cousin
Cousine (f)
(Gusinä)

Cousin
Cousin (m)
(Gusän)

Marital Status

Marital Status	Familiäschtand (m)		
single	ledig /single	**divorced**	gschidä
engaged	verlobt	**Widow**	Witwe (f)
married	verhüratet	**Widower**	Witwer (m)
separated	trännt	**widowed**	verwitwet

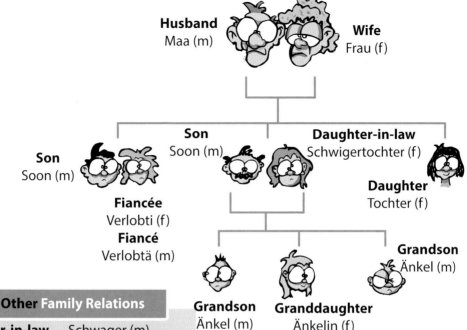

Husband
Maa (m)

Wife
Frau (f)

Son
Soon (m)

Son
Soon (m)

Daughter-in-law
Schwigertochter (f)

Fiancée
Verlobti (f)

Fiancé
Verlobtä (m)

Daughter
Tochter (f)

Grandson
Änkel (m)

Grandson
Änkel (m)

Granddaughter
Änkelin (f)

Other Family Relations

Brother-in-law	Schwager (m)
Father-in-law	Schwigervatter (m)
Grandchild	Gros-chind (n)
Mother-in-law	Schwigermuetter (f)
Nephew	Näffä (m)
Niece	Nichtä (f)
Relatives	Verwandti (pl)
Siblings	Gschwüschterti (pl)
Sister-in-law	Schwögerin (f)
Son-in-law	Schwigersoon (m)
Twins	Zwilling (pl)

People

Useful Family Terms

Family get together	Familiäzämäkunft (f)
	Familiäschluuch (m)
We are related.	Mir sind verwandt.
My family is important to me.	Mini Familiä isch mir wichtig.
I am a family person.	Ich bin än Familiämänsch.
My brother's name is…	Min Brüäder haisst…
Parent's home	Elterähuus (n)
My family lives in…	Mini Familiä läbt in…
Give my regards to your family.	Grüäss dini Familiä vo mir. (inf)
How is your family?	Wiä gat's dinerä Familiä? (inf)
We are going to have a baby!	Mir chömed äs Chind über!

Babies

Key survival words

baby	Beibi (n)	sleeper / "onesie"	Schtrampelazug (m),
baby bottle	Schoppä (m)		Schtramplär (m)
baby sling	Tragtuäch (n)	stuffed animal	Plüschtierli (n)
bedtime story	Guetnachtgschichtli(n)	swing	Giraitsi (pl) /
bib	Lazz (m)		Gigampfi (n)
changing table	Wikkeltisch (m)		Ritisaili (n)
cot / crib	Chinderbettli (n)	to bottle feed	dä Schoppä gä
dummy / pacifier	Nuggi (m)	to change a baby	Windlä wächslä
kindergarten	Chindsgi (m),	to count sheep	Schöfli zälä
	Chindergartä (m)	to nurse	schtilä
mash / baby food	Breili (n)	to suck one's thumb	am Tumä suggelä
nappies / diapers	Windlä (f/pl)	to teeth	zaanä
pediatrician	Chinderarzt (m) /	to vaccinate	impfä
	Chinderärztin (f)	to weep / to cry	brüälä, hülä
pram / stroller	Chinderwagä (m)	Twins	Zwilling (m/pl)

Key survival phrases

Do you have a fridge where I can store this milk?
Händ Sii än Chüälschrank, damit ich d'Milch uf-phaltä chann? (fr)
Could you please warm this bottle for me?
Chönd Sii mir dä Schoppä wärmä? (fr)
Where can I change the baby?
Wo chann ich mis Beibi wikklä?
Where can I nurse my baby in private?
Wo chann ich mis Beibi ungschtört schtillä?
Do you have a high chair?
Händ Sii än Hochschtuäl? (fr)
Where is the children's department?
Wo isch d'Chinderabteilig?
Is there a play ground close by?
Gitt's i dä Nächi än Schpillplazz?

Age

Baby boy
Büäbli (n)

Teenager
Teeni (m) (Tiini)

Boy
Buäb
(m)

Girl
Mait(ä)li (n)

Baby girl
Maitli (n)

Young man
Purscht (m)
jungä Maa (m)

Young woman
jungi Frau (f)
Frölain (n)

Adult
Erwachseni (f)

Old man
altä Maa (m)

Old woman
alti Frau (f)

Adult
Erwachsenä (m)

People

Home

House
Huus (n)

Chimney
Chämi (n)

Satellite Dish
Satellitäschüsslä (f)

Roof
Tach (n)

Tree
Baum (m)

Curtains
Vorhäng
(pl)

Wall
Wand
(f)

Window
Fänschter
(n)

Gutter
Tachrinnä (f)

Sunshade
Sunätach (n)

Door
Tüür (f)

Balcony
Balkon
(m)

Stairs
Schtägä
(f)

Mailbox
Briäfchaschtä (m)

Footpath
Wäg (m)

Garden
Gartä (m)

Lawn
Rasä (m)

Lawnmower
Rasämäier (m)

Housing

Parts of the House

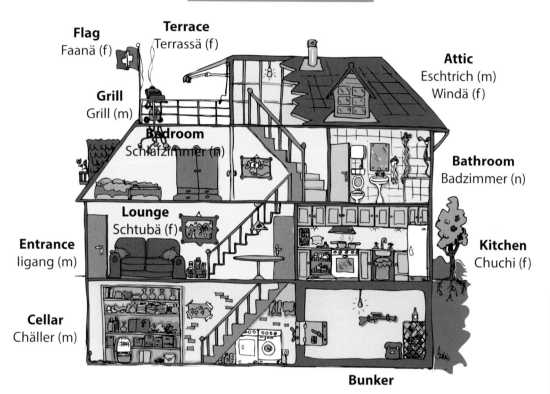

Flag
Faanä (f)

Terrace
Terrassä (f)

Attic
Eschtrich (m)
Windä (f)

Grill
Grill (m)

Bedroom
Schlafzimmer (n)

Bathroom
Badzimmer (n)

Lounge
Schtubä (f)

Entrance
Iigang (m)

Kitchen
Chuchi (f)

Cellar
Chäller (m)

Bunker
Luftschuzzchäller (m)

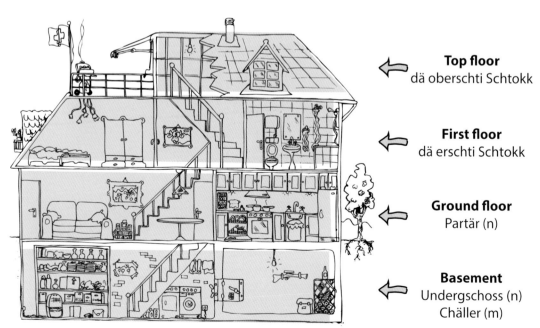

Top floor
dä oberschti Schtokk

First floor
dä erschti Schtokk

Ground floor
Partär (n)

Basement
Undergschoss (n)
Chäller (m)

Housing

99

Kitchen Utensils

Bowl	Schüsslä (f)	Pan	Pfanä (f)
Box	Schachtlä (f)	Dinner service	Tischset (n)
	Chischtä (f)	Spoon	Löffel (m)
Cup	Tassä (f)	Table mats	Tischmattä (f)
Cutlery	Pschtekk (n)	Table cloth	Tischtuäch (n)
Dishes	Gschirr (n)	Teaspoon	Teelöffeli (n)
Faucet / tap	Haanä (m)	Dishwasher	Abwäschmaschine (f)
Fork	Gablä (f)	Freezer	Tüfchüäler (m)
Frying pan	Bratpfanä (f)	Fridge	Chüälschrank (m)
Glass	Glas (n)	Rubbish bin	Apfall(chübel) (m)
Jam jar	Gomfiglas (n)	Microwave	Mikrowälä (f)
Kitchen shelves	Chuchiablagä (pl)	Oven	Ofä (m)
Knife	Mässer (n)	Stove	Härd (m)
Napkin	Serviettä (f)	Table	Tisch (m)
Plate	Täller (m)	Chair	Schtuäl (m)

Housing

Other House Areas

Entry way	Iigangshallä (f)	old building	Altbau (m)
Hallway	Gang (m)	new building	Noibau (m)
Lobby	Vorhallä (f)	Building	Geboide (n)
	Vorruum (m)	Garage	Garasch (f) (Garasch)
Dining room	Ässzimmer (n)	Basement garage	Tüüfgarage (f)
Floor	Bodä (m)		(Tüüfgarasch)
Utility room	Apschtellruum (m)	Children's room	Chinderzimmer (n)

WARNING !

In German speaking Switzerland, '**Zimmer**' refers to any other room than the kitchen or bathroom. So a '**Zwaizimmerwonig**' is a flat with a living room and one bedroom, a kitchen and a bathroom.

Housing

Toiletries

Body lotion	Körperlozioon (f)	*(Nessessär)*	
Brush	Bürschtä (f)	**Toilet paper**	WC-Papier (n)
Comb	Schträäl (m)		*(Weze-Papier)*
Deodorant	Deo (m)	**Toiletries**	Badzimmersachä (pl)
Hand cream	Handcreme (f)	**Toothbrush**	Zaabürschteli (n)
	(Handgräm)	**Toothpaste**	Zaapaschtä (f)
Make-up	Schminkzüg (n)	**Towel**	Tüächli (n)
Razor blades	Rasiärklingä (f)	**Shower**	Duschi (f)
Scales	Waag (f)	**Mirror**	Schpiägel (m)
Shampoo	Schampoo (n)	**Bath tub**	Badwannä (f)
Shower cream	Duschmittel (n)	**Washbasin**	Brüneli (n)
Soap	Soiffä (f)	**Shower curtain**	Duschvorhang (m)
Toiletry bag	Necessaire (n)		

Other Things in the House

Wardrobe	Gardärobä (f)	**Key**	Schlüssel (m)
Book shelves	Büächergschtell (n)	**Pillow**	Chüssi (n)
Carpet	Teppich (m)	**Plug**	Schtekker (m)
Closet	Chaschtä (m)	**Remote control**	Fernbediänig (f)
Desk	Pult (n)	**Sheet**	Bettuäch (n)
Drawer	Schubladä (f)	**Doorbell**	Huusgloggä (f)
Duvet	Bettdekki (f)	**Iron**	Bügälisä (n)
Hanger	Chlaiderbügel (m)		

Neighbours & Agencies

SWISS LAUNDRY SYSTEM

MORNING NEIGHBOUR !...

Housing

BE AWARE... Neighbours are usually quite friendly. You could engage in small talk using the different sections of this Survival Guide. Still, as it is common practice in older apartments to share all the laundry facilities with them, in most cases the laundry room might be the only place you communicate with your neighbours.

Looking for a Flat

Furnished room	möblierts Zimmer (f)
Furnished flat	möblierti Wonig (f)
Quiet area	ruigi Lag (f)
List of deficiencies	Mängellischtä (f)
I am looking for a cheap flat.	Ich suächä ä billigi Wonig.
Is the flat quiet / big / sunny?	Isch d'Wonig ruig / gross / sunig?
Do you have a flat for rent?	Händ Sii ä Wonig z'vermietä? (fr)
Do you know anybody who has a flat to rent?	Känned Sii öpper, wo ä Wonig z'vermietä hätt? (fr)
	Kännsch öpper, wo ä Wonig z'vermietä hätt? (inf)

Laundry

Detergent	Wöschmittel (n)
to iron	büglä
Laundry basket	Zaine (f)
Laundry	Wösch (f)
Laundry bag	Wöschsakk (m)
Laundry day	Wöschtag (m)
Laundry room	Wöschchuchi (f)
Laundry schedule	Wöschplan (m)
Tumble drier	Tumbler (m) *(Tömbler)*
washing	wäschä
Washing machine	Wöschmaschine (f)

Some Housing Words

Estate agency	Verwaltig (f)
Landlord	Vermieter (m)
	Vermieterin (f)
Tenant	Mieter (m)
	Mieterin (f)
One-room flat	Ainzimmerwonig (f)
Two-room flat	Zwaizimmerwonig (f)
Rental flat	Mietwonig (f)
Attic flat	Tachwonig (f)
	Attikawonig (f)
Neighbours	Nachbarä (pl)
Home owner	Huus-psizzer (m)
	Huus-psizzerin (f)
Two-level flat	Maisonette-Wonig (f)
	(Mäsonet-Wonig)

Housing

PERHAPS WE DIDN'T MAKE OURSELVES CLEAR AS TO THE DAY OF THE WEEK YOU SHOULD TAKE YOUR RUBBISH OUT

Neighbourly Survival Phrases (formal)

Please close the door!	Bitte mached Sii d'Huustür zuä! (fr)
Where can I throw my rubbish?	Wo chann ich dä Apfall hiituä?
Could you please keep the noise down?	Chönd Sii bitte echli ruig Sii? (fr)
I'm trying to sleep.	Ich möcht schlafä.
Would you like to come over for a coffee?	Möchtet Sii mal zu ois zum Kafi cho? (fr)
I'm your new neighbour.	Ich bin Irä noi Nachbar. (m) (fr)
	Ich bin Iri noi Nachbarin. (f) (fr)

Estate Agent Survival Phrases (formal)

I have problems with my neighbours.	Ich ha Problem / Krach mit dä Nachbarä
The... is not working.	Dä…isch kaputt
Please, can you send a repairman?	Chönd Sii bitte än Handwerker pschtelä? (fr)
When are we signing the contract?	Wänn chömmer dä Vertrag underschriibä?
I will move in, in...	Ich will im…iiziä.
I will move out in...	Ich will im…uusziä.
We need to check the inventory.	Mir müänd no äs Abgabeprotokoll machä.
It was like that when I moved in.	So hätt's usgsee, wo mir iizogä sind.

Questions You May Ask Your Landlord (formal)

How much is the rent?	Wiä höch isch d'Mieti?
What services are included with the rent?	Was isch i dä Mieti inbegriffä?
Do you have a cellar / attic /...?	Händ Sii än Chäller / ä Windä...? (fr)
How much is a parking space per month?	Wiä vill choschtet än Parkplazz pro Monät?
How long is the cancellation period?	Wiä lang isch Kündigungsfrischt?
Where can I do my laundry?	Wo channi mini Wösch wäschä?
When can I do my laundry?	Wänn chann ich wäschä?
Are pets allowed?	Sind Huustier erlaubt?
How much is the deposit?	Wiä hoch isch d'Kauzion?
Is there a school / playground nearby?	Hätt's ä Schuäl / än Schpillplazz i dä Nöchi?
Are you planning to raise the rent?	Planned Sii, d'Mieti z'erhöchä? (fr)
Can I paint the walls?	Chann ich d'Zimmer schtrichä?
When was the house renovated?	Wänn isch das Huus renoviert wordä?
When can I move in?	Wänn chann ich iiziä?
Can I use the terrace / garden?	Törf ich d'Terrassä / dä Gartä benuzzä?
How far is it to the next bus station?	Wiä wiit isch äs bis zur nächschtä Bus-schtazion?

BE AWARE... In Switzerland the landlord will always ask for a confirmation that you are in a good credit standing:

Chann ich än Betribigsuuszug ha?
(May I have a clearance certificate from the debt collection office?)

Questions Your Landlord May Ask You (formal)

Are you married?	Sind Sii verhüratet? (fr)
Do you have pets?	Händ Sii Huustier? (fr)
Yes, I have a dog / guinea pig.	Ja, ich ha än Hund / äs Meersoili.
Do you have a steady income?	Händ Sii än feschtä Loon? (fr)
How much do you earn?	Wiä vill verdiäned Sii? (fr)
I earn ... francs.	Ich verdiänä .... Frankä.
Do you have any children?	Händ Sii Chind? (fr)
How old are they?	Wiä alt sind diä?
Do you play an instrument?	Schpilled Sii äs Inschtrumänt? (fr)
Do you party a lot?	Mached Sii vill Partis? (fr)
Are you a foreigner?	Sind Sii Ussländer? (fr)
Where are you from?	Vo wo chömed Sii? (fr)
Have you ever been prosecuted?	Sind Sii je betribä wordä? (fr)
Do you smoke?	Rauched Sii? (fr)
Yes, I smoke.	Ja, ich rauchä.
No, I don't smoke.	Nai, ich rauchä nöd.

Numbers

BE AWARE... In Switzerland, digits are called **'Zalä'.** Number is **'Nummerä'** and refers to a set of digits, e.g. **Telefonnummerä** (phone number) or **Huusnummerä** (house number).

ais **1**	zwai **2**	drü **3**
vier **4**	foif **5**	sächs **6**
sibä **7**	acht **8**	nün **9**
*	null **0**	**#**

Schternzaichä (n)

Gartehaag (n)

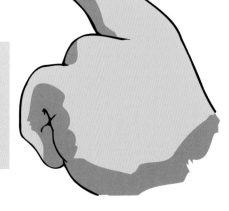

Ordinal Numbers

ten	zä
eleven	elf
twelve	zwölf
thirteen	drizä
fourteen	vierzä
fifteen	füfzä
sixteen	sächzä
seventeen	sibzä
eighteen	achzä
nineteen	nünzä
twenty	zwänzg
thirty	drissg
forty	vierzg
fifty	füfzg
sixty	sächzg
seventy	sibäzg
eighty	achtzg
ninety	nünzg
one hundred	hundert

Ordinal Numbers

two hundred	zwaihundert
one thousand	tuusig
two thousand	zwaituusig
hundred thousand	hunderttuusig
one million	Million (f)
one billion	Milliard (f)

Miscellaneous

Cardinal Numbers

first	erscht
second	zwait
third	dritt
fourth	viert
fifth	foift
sixth	sächst
seventh	sibät
eighth	acht
ninth	nünt
tenth	zät

BE AWARE... Numbers between 13 and 100 are always read from right to left (as in High German) so 21 is read **einäzwänzg** (one and twenty), 22 is **zwaiäzwänzg** (two and twenty), etc.

DON'T YOU WANT TO BE A MILLIONAIRE...?

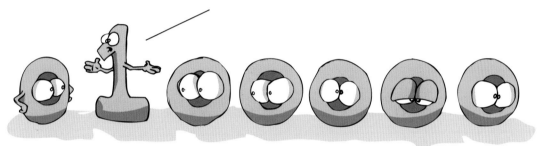

Other Numbers

even numbers	gradi Zaalä
odd numbers	ungradi Zaalä
Phone number	Telefonnummerä (f)
House number	Huusnummerä (f)
Insurance number	Versicherigsnummerä (f)
lucky number	Glükkszaal (f)
unlucky number	Unglükkszaal (f)
Code	Ghaimnummerä (f)
	Kod (m)
plus	und / plus
minus	minus
equals	isch glich/ git
Pension number	AHV *(Ahavau)-* Nummerä (f)

Toilets

Public Toilet Words

Toilet	Toilettä (f) *(Tualettä)*
	WC (n) *(Weze)*
Toilet paper	WC-Papier (n)
vacant	frei
occupied	psezt
Urinal	Pissoir (n) *(Pissuar)*
Washbasin	Lavabo (n) *(Lawabo)*
Soap	Soiffä (f)
Paper towel	Papiertuäch (n)
Hand dryer	Händtröchner (m)

TIP... Toilets in many public places are locked with a code system so that only the customers of the place can use them. On such occasions you can ask:

Wiä isch dä Kod für Toilettä / für's **WC?**
What is the code to open the toilet door?

Toilet Survival Phrases

Where is the toilet?	Wo isch s'WC *(Weze)*? Wo sind Toilettä *(Tualettä)*? Wo isch s'Hüüsli?
May I use your toilet?	Chann ich rasch uf d'Toilettä / uf s'WC?
Men's toilet	Mannätoilettä (pl)
Women's toilet	Frauätoilettä (pl)
Do you have any toilet paper?	Händ Sii WC-Papier? (fr) / Häsch WC-Papier? (inf)
Where is the toilet light?	Wo ischs WC-Liächt?

Miscellaneous

Education

Key survival words

Baccalaureate	Matur(a) (f)	**to learn**	leerä
pencil	Bleischtift (m/n)	**teacher**	Leerer (m)
book	Buäch (n)		Leererin (f)
fountain pen	Fülli (m)	**to cheat**	pschisä
primary school	Primar(schuäl) (f)	**to cram / to drill**	büfflä
Gymnasium	Gimi (n)	**recess / break**	Pausä (f)
high school	Sek(undarschuäl) (f)	**rubber / eraser**	Gummi (m)
homework	(Huus)ufgabä (pl)	**writing utensils**	Schriibzüg (n)
kindergarten	Chindsgi (m)	**school bag**	(Schuäler)thek (m)
day care	Chrippä (f)	**to cheat**	schpikkä / abluägä
biro / pen	Chugi (m)	**test**	Tescht (m)
exam	Prüäfig (f)	**university**	Uni(versität) (f)
to teach	lernä	**school report**	Zügnis (n)

General Non-Specific Terms

Generic Words

something	öppis
somewhere	noimät
somehow	irgendwiä
sometimes	mängisch
somebody	öpper
nothing	nüt
thing	Sach (f)
	Ding (n)
anything	irgendöppis

Generic Measures

long	lang
large	gross, äs 'L'(äl)
medium	mittler, äs 'M'(äm)
short	churz
wide	wiit
big	gross
small	chlii, äs 'S' (äs)

TIP... z' means 'too' in English and can be used with lots of adjectives **z'vill**, (too much / many) **z'wenig**, (too few / too little) **z'früä** (too early), **z'schpaat** (too late), **z'lang** (too long), etc.

Miscellaneous

Generic Time

moment	Momänt (m)
soon	bald
late	schpaat
early	früä
in a moment	grad / gli
now	jezt

Generic Quantity

more	mee
less / fewer	weniger
much / many	vill
too much	z'vill
too many	z'vill
few	wenig
a pair	äs paar
some	ainigi

Colours

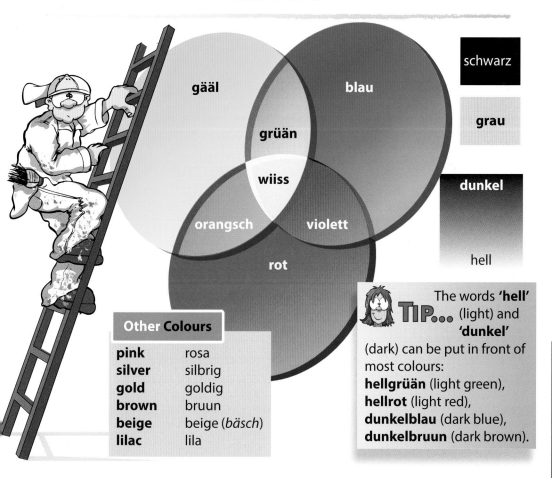

gääl

blau

grüän

wiiss

orangsch

violett

rot

schwarz

grau

dunkel

hell

Other Colours

pink	rosa
silver	silbrig
gold	goldig
brown	bruun
beige	beige (*bäsch*)
lilac	lila

TIP... The words **'hell'** (light) and **'dunkel'** (dark) can be put in front of most colours:
hellgrüän (light green),
hellrot (light red),
dunkelblau (dark blue),
dunkelbruun (dark brown).

Miscellaneous

✚ Swiss Expressions related to colours ✚

Literal translation	Meaning	Sentence in Swiss German
green behind the ears	(immature)	grüän hinder dä Oorä
to have a green thumb	(to be good with plants)	än grüänä Tumä
to see it black	(to be pessimistic)	schwarz gsee
Black market	(illegal market)	Schwarzmärt (m)
a golden hand	(a lucky hand)	ä goldigi Hand
A white waistcoat	(innocent)	ä wiissi Weschtä
to be 'blue'	(to be drunk)	blau / er isch blau
A grey mouse	(a person that no one notices)	äs graus Müsli
to see things in pink clouds	(to be naïve)	dur ä rosaroti Brülä gsee

Animals

Bird
Vogel (m)

Fish
Fisch (m)

Bee
Biändli (n)
Biänä (f)

Fly
Flügä (f)

Ostrich
Schtrauss (m)

Horse
Ross (n)

Cow
Chuä (f)

Crocodile
Krokodil (n)

Cat
Chazz (f)
Büsi (n)

Snake
Schlangä (f)

Turkey
Truuthaan (m)

Pig
Sau (f)

Dog
Hund (m)

Chicken
Huän (n)

Rabbit
Chüngel (m)

Penguin
Pinguin (m)

Duck
Äntä (f)

Lamb
Lamm (n)

Turtle
Schildchrot (f)

Miscellaneous

Alpine Wildlife

Buzzard	Moisebussard (m)
Chamois	Gäms (f)
Deer	Hirsch (m)
Eagle	Adler (m)
European ibex	Schtaibokk (m)
Fox	Fuchs (m)
Jackdaw	Doolä (f)
Lynx	Luchs (m)
Marmot	Murmeli (n)
	Murmeltiär (n)
	Munggä (m)
Marten	Marder (m)
Mouse	Muus (f) / Müsli (n)
Roe deer	Ree (n)
Wild boar	Wildsau (f)
Wolf	Wolf (m)

Other Animals

Bear	Bär (m)
Bull	Schtiär (m)
Donkey	Esel (m)
Elephant	Elefant (m)
Goat	Gaiss (f)
Guinea pig	Meersoili (n)
Hippopotamus	Nilpferd (n)
	Flusspferd (n)
Lion	Loi (m)
Lizard	Aidächsli (n)
Monkey	Aff (m)
Rhinoceros	Nashorn (n)
Rooster	Güggel (m)
Tiger	Tiger (m)
Zebra	Zebra (n)

Bugs / Insects

Bug	Wanzä (f)	Worm	Wurm (m)
Insect	Insekt (n)	Wasp	Wäschpi (n)
Beetle	Chäfer (m)	Cockroach	Kakerlakä (f)
Fly	Flügä (f)	Ant	Amaisä (f)
Mosquito	Muggä (f)	Butterfly	Schmätterling (m)
Slug	Schnägg (m)		Summervogel (m)
Spider	Schpinä (f)		

Miscellaneous

Time

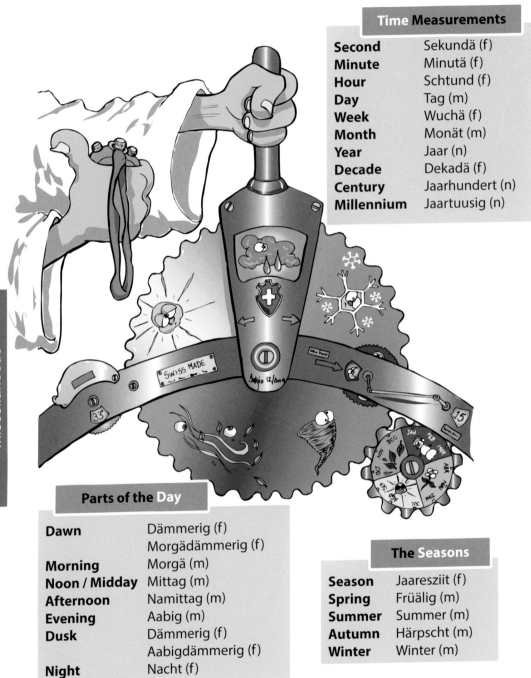

Time Measurements

Second	Sekundä (f)
Minute	Minutä (f)
Hour	Schtund (f)
Day	Tag (m)
Week	Wuchä (f)
Month	Monät (m)
Year	Jaar (n)
Decade	Dekadä (f)
Century	Jaarhundert (n)
Millennium	Jaartuusig (n)

Parts of the Day

Dawn	Dämmerig (f)
	Morgädämmerig (f)
Morning	Morgä (m)
Noon / Midday	Mittag (m)
Afternoon	Namittag (m)
Evening	Aabig (m)
Dusk	Dämmerig (f)
	Aabigdämmerig (f)
Night	Nacht (f)

The Seasons

Season	Jaaresziit (f)
Spring	Früälig (m)
Summer	Summer (m)
Autumn	Härpscht (m)
Winter	Winter (m)

Miscellaneous

Moments in Time

Past	vergangä
	Vergangähait (f)
Present / now	jezt
	Gägäwart (f)
Future	Zuäkumft (f)
	zuäkümftig
Yesterday	geschter
Today	hüt
Tomorrow	morn
Weekend	Wuchänänd (n)
the day before yesterday	vorgeschter
the day after tomorrow	übermorn

Key Survival Phrases

What time is it?	Wiä schpaat isch äs?
	Was isch für Ziit?
At what time...?	Wänn…?
When do we meet?	Wänn träffämmär ois?
When do you go to..?	Wänn gönd Sii uf..? (fr)
	Wänn gasch uf…? (inf)
Sorry, I am late.	Tuät mir Laid, ich bi z'schpaat.
I will be 10 minutes late.	Ich chumä zä Minutä z'schpaat.
What day is today?	Welä Tag hämmer hüt?
	Was isch hüt für än Tag?
When is that?	Wänn isch das?
From when / until when?	Vo wänn / bis wänn?
exactly	genau
Do you have time?	Händ Sii Ziit? (fr)
	Häsch Ziit? (inf)
every week	jedi Wuchä
every month / every year	jedä Monät / jedäs Jaar
When does the film start?	Wänn fangt dä Film aa?
When does the film finish?	Wänn hört dä Film uf?
How long does the film last?	Wiä lang gat dä Film?
	Wiä lang durät dä Film?
The film starts at...	Dä Film fangt am … aa.
The film finishes at...	Dä Film hört am … uf.

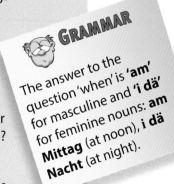

GRAMMAR

The answer to the question 'when' is **'am'** for masculine and **'i dä'** for feminine nouns: **am Mittag** (at noon), **i dä Nacht** (at night).

Miscellaneous

Days of the Week

Monday	Mäntig
Tuesday	Ziischtig
Wednesday	Mittwuch
Thursday	Dunnschtig
Friday	Friitig
Saturday	Samschtig
Sunday	Sunntig

Months of the Year

January	Januar (m)
February	Februar (m)
March	März (m)
April	April (m)
May	Mai (m)
June	Juni (m)
July	Juli (m)
August	Auguscht (m)
September	Septämber (m)
October	Oktober (m)
November	Novämber (m)
December	Dezämber (m)

 TIP... Although most Swiss have a watch, sometimes you will be asked by strangers **'Händ Sii ä Uur?'** (Do you have a watch?) This question means: What time is it?

 TIP... To indicate time, the preposition **am** is used: **am drü,** means at three, **am sächsi** means at 6 o'clock.

 GRAMMAR

All the months, days of the week and the seasons are masculine, which means that **dä** is used: **dä Januar, dä Mäntig, dä Früälig**).

116

Telling Time

| sächsi | föif ab sächsi | zä ab sächsi | Viertel ab sächsi | zwänzg ab sächsi |

| Föif vor halbi sibni (literarlly: 'five before half seven') | halbi sibni | föif ab halbi sibni (literally: 'five after half seven') |

| zwänzg vor sibni | Viertel vor sibni | zä vor sibni | föif vor sibni | sibni |

Miscellaneous

Before **vor** **ab** After

Weather & Temperature

TIP... Weather is the number one small-talk topic in Switzerland. It is often used as a topic to start a conversation.

Miscellaneous

Key Survival Phrases

The sun is shining.	D'Sunä schiint.
It's raining.	Äs rägnät.
It's snowing.	Äs schnait.
It's chilly/foggy/humid.	Äs isch chüäl/näblig/füächt.
It's going to rain.	Äs chunnt go rägnä.
Today it's very warm / cold.	Hüt isch äs warm / chalt.
It's getting chilly.	Äs wird chüäl.
Summer is coming.	Dä Summer chunnt.
The weather is improving.	Äs tuät uf.
warm wind coming from the south	Föön (m) *(Foehn)*
What is the weather forecast for tomorrow?	Wiä isch dä Wätterpricht für morn?

Weather & Temperature

Climate	Klima (n)	**Lightning**	Blizz (m)
cloudy	wolkig / bedekkt	**Rain**	Räge (m) / rägnä
sunny	sunig	**Snow**	Schnee (m)
cold	chalt	**Storm**	Schturm (m)
cool	chüel	**Sun**	Sunä (f)
dry	trochä	**Temperature**	Temperatur (f)
Fog	Näbel (m)	**Thunder**	Tunner (m)
Forecast	Wätterpricht (m)	**Thunderstorm**	Gwitter (n)
Hail	Hagel (m) / haglä	**warm**	warm
Heat	Hizz (f)	**Weather**	Wätter (n)
hot	haiss	**Weather report**	Wätterpricht (m)
humid	füecht	**Wind**	Wind (m)

BE AWARE... The 'weather verbs' (**rägnä, schneiä,** etc.) always need the impersonal subject **äs**, **äs rägnät** (it's raining).

Miscellaneous

Part III

Decoding the Swiss

Swiss 'Slanguage'

This last part of the Survival Guide presents some of the key Swiss German words and expressions which are often used in an informal environment. These are used by people of all social classes and ages, but it is the younger generation that may be found using the 'slanguage' more often.

The origin of the Swiss 'slanguage' varies: some words are typical Swiss words that have adopted a new meaning, metaphorical in some cases (**D'Ufzgi sind schoggi** – The homework is easy). Some other words are foreignisms, which means that the word is peculiar to a foreign language, but the grammatical pattern follows the Swiss German one. In particular the influence of the American and British culture, which is quite strong, plays an important role in younger people's words and expressions (**foodä** for eat).

Language Evolution

As with fashion, Swiss words keep evolving and changing; the words used today could possibly change their spelling or meaning tomorrow.

Because it is a 'moving target', it is advisable to keep track of the type of Swiss German the people around you are using, and try to adapt to it.

Slang Words (especially in Zurich)

A

abtubä	to run away
än Abgang machä	to leave
Äs isch voll abgangä.	It was exciting.
abtanzä	to dance non-stop
abtrukkä	pay
achozzä	to be reluctant to do something
anderscht (mega)	very
aaschiissä	not in the mood for something

B

bö	no idea
Bonapp	Enjoy your meal
Buddle (f)	a bottle
büglä	to work

C

Chämi (n)	heavy smoker
Chazz (f)	attractive woman
chisä	to throw up
Chischtä (f)	a million francs
chluppä	to steal
chnüttlä	to work hard
Cholä (m)/ Chlozz (m)	money

D

derb	bad, disgusting (*also*: great, fantastic)
De/diä chasch rauche	he/she is an idiot

Continued on the next page...

Slang Words (especially in Zurich)

E		**huerä**	extremely
ebä	that's what I said, exactly	**Huscheli (n)**	a wall flower
		I	
F		**inäbiigä**	to eat
fägä	to take great pleasure	**Isch buechet**	it's a deal
filzä	to frisk, to shake down		
foodä (fuudä)	to eat something	**J**	
fridlich	peaceful, comfortable	**jentschtes / jeni**	a lot of something
Frittä (f)	hairstyle		
fuulä Sakk	sluggard	**K**	
		voll krass	very cool
G		**kuul**	cool
gäch	great, brilliant	**än Knall ha /**	crazy
gedigä	comfortable	**än Eggäab ha**	
H		**L**	
hängä / umehängä	to spend time somewhere or with someone	**Lappä (m)**	100 francs
		Lungebröötli (n)	cigarette
hammer	super		
Hänger (m)	a lazy person		

Continued on the next page...

Slang Words (especially in Zurich)

M

mega	extremely, super
muffä	to stink
muggä	to steal

P

Puff (n)	disorder

S

scheikä	to dance
schiäf	odd, strange
schlotä	to smoke heavily
Schnügel (m)	nice looking guy
scho	OK, of course
schoggi	easy
än Schönä	have a nice day/ evening
schpüälä	to forget, to fail
schräg	odd, strange
Schtuzz	money
(än mega) Schuss	attractive woman
Servelapromi (m)	c-list celebrity
so z'vill	superfluous
Suchthuufä (m)	person with addictive behaviour
suuffä	to drink a lot

T

tscheggä	to understand

Turi (m) — a tourist
tschillä — to cool off, to relax

U

us-tiggä	to go mad, to go crazy

V

verarschä	to cheat on somebody
verbokkä	fail
verbrächä	make a stupid mistake
verhäderet	confusing, entangled
verhängä	to forget
verhängt	missed (opportunity)
verhängtä Siäch	person who doesn't care about anything
(a Prüefig) verhauä	to fail (a test)
versiächä	to fail, to forget
versiffä	to miss out on something
voll edel	really nice, beautiful

W

waisch wo?	certainly not !
Was gaat ap?	What's up?

Z

ziä	buy, have a drink
zupfä	to leave

125

Swiss Idioms

Sayings and expressions are a key part of the linguistic heritage of a society. They are very interesting since they reflect, in a playful way, a lot about the social culture, and the Swiss are quite creative when it comes to using them.

As a final point, we would like to introduce some of these Swiss sayings and expressions. Comparing them with the ones used in other countries, one can find some similarities in the metaphorical meaning as well as with the expression itself; however, the majority of them are unique to Swiss German.

Swiss Idiom	Literal Translation	Meaning
Er isch uusgraschtet.	He freaked out.	He freaked out.
Sii hätt ä langi Laitig.	She has a long cable.	She is slow to catch the meaning.
ufs Gratwool	on the off chance	on the off chance
Da lit dä Hund begrabä.	That's where the dog is buried.	the crux of the matter
Das isch kais Honigschläkkä.	It's not a honey lick.	It's difficult.
nümmä alli Tassä im Schrank	not all cups in the cupboard / S/he's missing cups in his/her cupboard.	crazy
Sii isch rächt blauoigig.	She is blue-eyed.	She is naive.
Das isch kain Schläkk.	That's not a lick.	It's difficult.
s'hinterletscht	The last thing	last thing possible / the worst thing
Er kännt nüt.	He doesn't know anything.	He goes for it despite the odds.
Sii/Er hätt alles gä.	S/he gave everything.	S/he put in a maximum of effort.
Er isch scharf uf sii.	He is hot on her.	He fancies her (sexually).
vo Tutä und Blasä kai Aanig	no idea about hooting nor blowing	Really naïve / uninformed
ufläsä	to scrape	to pick up
ä schpizzi Zungä	A pointed tongue	straight to the point
Er hätt's sii abgschleppt.	He towed her away.	He seduced her and took her home.

Swiss Idiom	Literal Translation	Meaning
Häsch än Knall?	Do you have a bang?	Are you crazy?
Bisch durä bi rot?	Have you crossed on red?	Have you lost your mind?
Ais um s'ander wiä z'Paris.	One thing after another, just like in Paris	one thing after another
än Schprung i dä Schüsslä	a crack in the bowl	crazy
Gat's no!	No way!	No way!
Ämenä gschänktä Gaul luägt mär nöd is Muul.	Don't look a gifted horse in the mouth.	If it's a gift, don't criticize it.

Swiss Idiom	Literal Translation	Meaning
ufglaisä	to rerail	initiate
Ich drukk dir dä Tumä.	I press my thumb for you.	I will be thinking of you / wish you good luck.
Diä / Dä chammer dä Buggel aberutschä.	S/he can slide down my hump.	I don't care at all about her/him.
Sii / Er macht kain Wank.	S/he doesn't move.	S/he doesn't move or make a sound.
Hans was Hairi.	John is like Henry.	It's all the same.
Sii / Er macht d'Fuscht im Sakk.	S/he is making a fist in the pocket.	S/he is secretly angry.
Cervelat-Promi	sausage VIP Starlet	a would-like-to-be famous person
Schikki-Mikki	chic person	posh person
Sii haltet zäme wiä Päch und Schwefel.	They stick together like pitch and sulphur.	They are inseparable friends.
Sii / Er faart voll uf das ab.	S/he drives completely after this.	S/he is very much into this.
Sii / Er wott dä Foifer und s'Weggli.	S/he wants the penny and the roll.	S/he wants everything.
Sii / Er schwümmt im Gäld.	S/he is swimming in money.	S/he is very rich.
schaffä wiä än Tubel	work like a madman	work a lot
än Chazzäschprung	only a cat jump	only a few blocks away
Jezt chumm ich drus.	I'm coming out.	Now I understand.
wiä äs Lama	just like a lama	very slow

Frequent Confusions

"When Swiss people speak High German you can usually immediately recognise them as being Swiss because of their accent and the way they construct their sentences. And of course there is their special vocabulary. In 'Helvetic' High German dialect words are often just adapted to the High German phonology

which is correct most of the time but in some cases causes confusion for Germans since some Helvetic words do not have a direct equivalent in High German. Furthermore, the influence of French and other Romanic languages is stronger in Switzerland than in Germany. This means there are three versions: Swiss German, Helvetic German and Standard (High) German. On the following pages you'll find some words that will either cause confusion or amusement in Germany."

Confusing words

English	High German	in using High German a Swiss will say ... (Helvetic German)	Züridütsch
address	Anschrift	Adresse	Adrässä (f)
agenda item	Tagesordnungspunkt	Traktandum	Traktandum (n)
appear (verb)	den Anschein haben	Den Anschein machen	dä Aaschii machä
attic	Dachstock (m)	Estrich	Eschtrich (m)
bag for toiletries	Kulturbeutel	Necessaire	Nessessär (n)
beet	Rote Beete	Randen	Randä (m)
bicycle	Fahrrad	Velo	Welo (n)
blond highlights	Blonde Strähnchen	Mèches	Mäsch (pl)
blow (verb)	wehen	winden	windä
breakfast	Frühstück	Morgenessen	Zmorgä (m)
building superintendent	Hausmeister	Abwart	Abwaart (m)

Confusing words

English	High German	in using High German a Swiss will say ... (Helvetic German)	Züridütsch
carpet	Teppichboden	Spannteppich	Spannteppich (m)
carrot	Karotte	Rübli	Rüäbli (n)
closet	Schrank	Kasten	Chaschtä (m)
conductor	Schaffner	Kondukteur	Kondiktör (m)
contemplate (verb)	nachdenken	studieren	studiärä
courgette	Zucchini	Zuchetti	Zuggetti (f)
crate for drinks	Getränkekiste	Harass	Harass (m)
cream	Sahne	Rahm	Raam (m)
debt collection	Schuldeneintreibung	Betreibung	Betribig (f)
deposit	Pfand	Depot	Debbo (n)
desk	Schreibtisch	Pult	Pult (n)
driver	Fahrer	Chauffeur	Schofför (m)/Schoffös (f)
fireplace	Kamin	Cheminée	Schminee (n)
evening meal	Abendessen	Znachtessen	Znacht (m)
funeral service	Trauerfeier	Abdankung	Abdankig (f)
get rid of (verb)	loswerden	abschieben	abschiäbä
get undressed (verb)	sich ausziehen / sich auskleiden	sich abziehen	sich abziä
go out (verb)	ausgehen / abends weggehen	in den Ausgang gehen	in Usgang ga
go shopping (verb)	einkaufen / shoppen	lädeln	lädälä
grapefruit	Pampelmuse (f)	Grapefruit	Gräpfrü (f)
grill (verb)	grillen	grillieren	grilliärä
hairdresser	Friseur	Coiffeur	Guafför (m), Coiffös (f)
handkerchief	Taschentuch	Nastuch	Nastüächli (n)
helicopter	Hubschrauber	Helikopter	Heli(kopter) (m)
hen	Huhn	Poulet	Pulle (n)
hospital	Krankenhaus	Spital	Spital (n/m)
ice cream	Eis	Glacé	Glasse (m)
ID	Personalausweis	Identitätskarte (ID)	Ii-Dee (f)
insinuate (verb)	andeuten	antönen	atönä
interruption	Unterbrechung	Unterbruch	Underbruch (m)
iron (verb)	bügeln	glätten	glettä
lamb's lettuce	Feldsalat	Nüsslisalat	Nüsslisalat (m)
lorry / truck	Lastwagen	Camion	Laschtwagä (m)
mailman	Postbote	Pöstler	Pöschtlär (m)/Pöschtlerin (f)
make an appointment (verb)	sich verabreden	abmachen	abmachä
mascara	Wimperntusche	Mascara	Maskara (f)
mess	Unordnung	nicht aufgeräumt	Puff (n) (colloquial)
motorcycle	Motorrad	Töff	Töff (m)
move house (verb)	umziehen	zügeln	züglä
on the other hand	andererseits	handkehrum	handkerum

Confusing words

English	High German	in using High German a Swiss will say ... (Helvetic German)	Züridütsch
pant's fly	Hosenschlitz	Hosenladen	Hosäladä (m)
paprika	Paprika	Peperoni	Pepperooni (m)
park (verb)	parken	parkieren	parkierä
parking ticket	Strafzettel	Busse	Puäss (f)
pavement / sidewalk	Gehsteig	Trottoir	Trottuar (n)
peanuts	Erdnüsse	Spanische Nüsse	spanischi Nüssli (pl)
penthouse / loft	Penthouse	Attikawohnung	Attikawoonig (f)
perch	Barsch	Egli	Egli (m)
perfect	perfekt	pico bello	piggo bello
plastic folder	Aktenhülle	Sichtmäppchen	Sichtmäppli (n)
platform / track	Bahnsteig	Perron	Perron (n)
pocket knife	Taschenmesser	Sackmesser	Sakkmässär (n)
possibly	etwaig	allfällig	allfällig
proposition	Angebot	Offerte	Offärtä (f)
purse / wallet	Geldbeutel	Portmonee	Portmonee (n)
ring (verb)	klingeln	läuten	lüütä
rustic	urig	urchig	urchig
scooter (with motor)	Roller	Vespa	Weschpa(f)
scooter (no motor)	Tretroller	Trotinett	Trotinett (n)
secondhand shop	Gebrauchtwarenladen	Brokenhaus	Brokkähuus (n)
service / tip	Bedienung	Service	Serwiss (m)
shoestring	Schnürsenkel	Schuhbändel	Schuäbändäl (m/pl)
sit down (verb)	sich setzen	absitzen	absizzä
ski boot	Skistiefel	Skischuhe	Schiischuä (m)
skirt	Rock (m)	Jupe	Schüpp (m)
slippers	Hausschuhe	Finken	Fingkä (m/pl)
soon	innerhalb des Zeitrahmens	innert nützlicher Frist	innert nüzzlicher Frischt
sound (verb)	klingen	tönen	töönä
spicy hot	scharf (gewürzt)	rassig	rassig
stapler	Tacker	Bostitch	Posttitsch (m)
stationer's	Schreibwarengeschäft	Papeterie	Babbeterii (f)
strong-flavoured	würzig (Käse)	rezent	rezänt
suit jacket	Sakko / Anzugsjacke	Tschoppen	Tschoppä (m)
tabletop soccer	Tischfussball spielen	töggeln	töggelä
telephone (verb)	anrufen	ein Telefon geben	äs Telefon gä/telefoniärä
telephone (verb)	anrufen	anläuten	aalütä
there is	es gibt	es hat	es hätt
ticket	Fahrkarte (f)	Billet	Billet (m)
toboggan / sled	rodeln	schlitteln	schlittlä
touch (verb)	berühren	anlangen	aalangä
tough	zäh (metaphorisch benutzt)	harzig	harzig
traffic light	Verkehrsampel	Lichtsignal	Signaal (n)/Liächtsignal (n)
tram / streetcar	Strassenbahn	Tram	Tram (n)
tuna	Thunfisch	Thon	Ton (m)

Confusing words

English	High German	in using High German a Swiss will say ... (Helvetic German)	Züridütsch
vest	Weste	Gilet	Schile (m)
vote (verb)	seine Stimme abgeben/ wählen	stimmen / wählen	(ab)schtimmä/wäälä
walnut	Walnuss	Baumnuss	Baumnuss (f)
washbasin	Waschbecken	Lavabo	Lawaboo (n)
wipe (verb)	kehren	wischen	wüschä
with the naked eye	mit blossem Auge	von Auge	vo Aug
within	innerhalb von (Zeitspanne)	innert	innert
work (verb)	arbeiten	schaffen	schaffä

BE AWARE... Swiss German is very precise in certain aspects. For example, there are very different terms for the concept of work, depending on how it is performed:

schaffä	work
schäffälä	do easy work
chrampfä	toil
büglä	work (colloquial)
chnüttlä	toil
pfuschä	work carelessly
werchlä	do easy work
fuhrwerchlä	piddle around
büäzä	do manual work
juflä	work carelessly
lauärä	dally
schwadlä	work carelessly
übertuä	overdo oneself
grümschälä	pretend to work

IS EVERYTHING CLEAR...?

Appendix

Pronouns and Articles

Personal Pronouns

	1st person	2nd person	3rd person
nom, sg.	ich	du	er
acc. sg.	mich	di	in
dat. sg.	mir	dir	im
nom. pl.	mir	ier	sii
acc. pl.	ois	oi	sii
dat. pl,	ois	oi	inä

Indefinite Articles

	masculine	feminine	neuter
common case	än	ä	äs
dative case	ämä (n), ämänä(n)	ärä(n), änärä(n)	ämä(n), ämänä(n)

Definite Articles

	masculine	feminine	neuter	plural
common case	dä	d, di	s	d, di
dative case	äm	där	äm	dä

Demonstrative Pronouns

	masculine	feminine	neuter	plural
common case	dä	die	das	die
	desäb	disäb	säb	disäbe
dative case	däm	däre	däm	däne
	säbem	säbere	säbem	säbe
	emsäbe(n)	dersäbe	emsäbe	desäbe

Possessive Pronouns

	masculine	feminine	neuter	plural
common case	min	mini	mis	mini
dative case	mim	minärä	mim	minä
common case	din	dinerä	dis	dini
dative case	dim	dinerä	dim	dinä
common case	sin	sinä	sis	sini
dative case	sim	sinerä	sim	sinä
common case	oise(n)	oisä	oisäs	oisi
dative case	oisem	oisere	oisem	oise
common case	oie(n)	oii	oies	oii
dative case	oisem	oiere	oiem	oie(n)
common case	ire(n)	iri	ires	iri
dative case	irem	irärä	iräm	irä

Verbs

There is neither a simple past nor a past perfect in Swiss German.

BE AWARE...

Survival Verbs

	inf.	ich	du	er	mir	ier	sii
be	si	bi	bisch	isch	sind	sind	sind
become	werde	wird	wirsch	wird	wärded	wärded	wärded
come	cho	chumm	chunsch	chunnt	chömmed	chömmed	chömmed
do	tuä	tuä	tuäsch	tuät	tüänd	tüänd	tüänd
drink	trinkä	trinkä	trinksch	trinkt	drinked	drinked	drinked
drive	faarä	faarä	faarsch	faart	faaret	faaret	faaret
eat	ässä	ässä	issisch	isst	ässed	ässed	ässed
give	ge	gibä	gisch	git	gänd	gänd	gänd
go	gaa	gang	gasch	gat	gönd	gönd	gönd
have	ha	ha	häsch	hätt	händ	händ	händ
hear	losä	losä	losisch	losed	losed	losed	losed
hold	hebä	hebä	hebsch	hebt	hebed	hebed	hebed
like	gärn ha	ha gärn	häsch gärn	er hät gärn	händ gärn	händ gärn	händ gärn
love	liäbä	liäbä	liäbsch	liäbt	liäbed	liäbed	liäbed
say	sägä	sägä	säisch	säit	säged	säged	säged
see	luägä	luägä	luägsch	luägt	luäged	luäged	luäged
sleep	schlafä	schlafä	schlafsch	schlaft	schlafed	schlafed	schlafed
travel	raisä	raisä	raisisch	raist	raised	raised	raised
walk	lauffä	lauffä	lauffsch	laufft	lauffed	lauffed	lauffed
want	welä	will	willsch	will	wännd	wännd	wännd
wash	wäschä	wäschä	wäschisch	wäsched	wäsched	wäsched	wäsched
work	schaffä	schaffä	schaffisch	schafft	schaffed	schaffed	schaffed

Other Common Past Tenses (Perfect tense)

Ich bi gsi	**I have been / I was**
Ich ha gmacht	**I have made / I made**
Ich ha trunkä	**I have drunk / I drank**
Ich ha gässä	**I have eaten / I ate**
Ich ha gschlafä	**I have slept / I slept**
Ich bi gloffä	**I have walked / I walked**
Ich bi gangä	**I have gone / I went**
Ich ha glosed	**I have listened / I listened**
Ich ha gschaffed	**I have worked / I worked**
Ich bi gfaarä	**I have driven / I drove**
I ha gluäged	**I have watched / I watched**

TIP... The past in German is built with the verb **ha** (have) + the past participle:

Ich ha d'Ufzgi gmacht
(I did my homework).

Some verbs (usually movements) build the past with the verb **si** (to be) + the past participle:

Ich bin uf Züri gangä
(I went to Zurich).

Modal Verbs

	Inf	1 pres	2 pres	pl. pres	subj.	cond.
can	chönä	cha	chasch	chönd	chönn	chönd
like	mögä	mag	magsch	möge	mög	möcht
may	törffä	törff	törfsch	törffed	törffi	törft
must	müäsä	muäs, muän	muäsch	müänd	müäs	müässt
should	sölä	söll	sölsch	söled	söll	sött
want	welä	wott, will	wotsch	wänd	well	wett

The Dictionary
English – Swiss German
Swiss German – English

English - Swiss German

A

Abdomen	Buuch (m)
above (prep)	über
Abscess	Apszäss (m)
according to (prep)	nach
across (prep)	über
across from (prep)	gägänüber
Address	Adrässä (f)
Address book	Addrässbuäch (n)
Adult	Erwachsenä/i (m/f)
Advertising	Wärbig (f)
Aeroplane	Flugzüg (n)
afraid	ängschtlich
after (prep)	nach
Afternoon	Namittag (m)
against (prep)	gägä
Airmail	Luftposcht (f)
allergic to	alergisch gägä
Allergy	Alergii (f)
along (prep)	entlang
Alpenhorn	Alphorn (m)
amazed	erschtunt
Ambulance	Ambulanz (f), Chrankäwagä (m)
angry	bös
Ankle	Chnöchel (m)
Answering machine	Telefonbeantworter(m)
Ant	Amaisä (f)
Antidote	Gägägift (n)
anxious	ängschtlich
anything	irgendöppis
Appendicitis	Blinddarmenzündig (f), Süassmoscht (m)
Apple	Öpfel (m)
Apple juice	Öpfelsaft (m)
Appointment	Termin (m)
Appraisal	Quali(fikation) (f) , Laischtigsbewärtig (f)
Apprentice	Leerling (m)
April	April (m)
Area code	Vorwaal (f)

argue (verb)	schtriitä
Argument	Schtriit (m)
Arm	Arm (m)
around (prep)	um
Arrival	Akunft (f)
Article	Artikel (m)
Art	Kunscht (f)
Aspirin	Aschpirin (n)
Assistant	Asischtänt/in (m/f)
Asthma	Aschtma (n)
at (prep)	bi / am
Attachment	Attachment (n) (Attätschmänt)
Attic	Eschtrich (m), Windä (f)
Attic flat	Tachwonig (f), Attikawonig (f)
August	Auguscht (m)
Aunt	Tantä (f)
Autumn	Härpscht (m)
Avalanche	Lawinä (f)

B

B	B&B (n)
B&B	B&B (n)
Baby boy	Büäbli (n)
Baby girl	Maitli (n)
Back	Ruggä (m)
Bacon	Schpäkk (m)
bad	schlächt
bad luck	Päch (m)
Baguette	Pariserbrot (n)
Bakery	Bekk (m), Bekkerei (f)
Balcony	Balkon (m)
Banana	Bananä (f)
Bandage	Verband (m)
Band-aid	Pfläschterli (n)
Bank	Bank (f)
Bank account	Bankkonto (n)
Banknote	Banknotä (f)
Bar	Bar (f)
Barbecue	Grillfäscht (n)
Basement	Undergschoss (n)
Basement garage	Tüfgarasch (f)

Bath tub	Badwannä (f)
Bathroom	Badzimmer (n)
Beach	Schtrand (m)
Beans	Boonä (f)
Bear	Bär (m)
beautiful	schön
Bed	Bett (n)
Bed cover	Bettaazug (m)
Bedroom	Schlafzimmer (n)
Bee	Biändli (n), Biinä (f)
Beef	Rindflaisch (n), Biär (n)
Beetle	Chäfer (m)
behind (prep)	hinder
beige	beige (bäsch)
Bellybutton	Buchnabel (m)
Belt	Gürtel (m), Gurt (m)
beneath (prep)	under
beside (prep)	näbäd
between (prep)	zwüschä
big	gross
billion	Milliard (f)
Bird	Vogel (m)
Birthday party	Geburtstags-party (f)
bitter	bitter
black	schwarz
blink (verb)	blinzlä
Blood	Bluät (n)
Blood pressure	Bluätdrukk (m)
Blood sugar	Bluätzukker (m)
Blouse	Blusä (f)
blow (verb)	blasä
blue	blau
Board of Directors	Verwaltigsrat (m)
Body lotion	Körperlozioon (f)
boiled	gkocht
Bonus	Bonus (m)
Book	Buäch (n)
Book shelves	Büächergschtell (n)
Bookshop	Büächhandlig (f), Büächerladä (m)
Border	Gränzä (f)
bored	glangwiilet
Boss	Chef/in (m/f) (Schef/in)

Bottom	Füdli (n)
Bowl	Schüsslä (f)
Box	Schachtlä (f), Chischtä (f)
Boy	Buäb (m)
Bra	Beha (m)
Brand	Markä (f)
Bread	Brot (n)
Break	Pausä (f)
Breakfast	Zmorgä (m)
Breast	Busä (m)
Bridge	Brugg (f)
Briefcase	Arbetsmappä (f)
Broccoli	Broggoli (m)
Broken bone	Chnochäbruch (m)
Brother	Brüäder (m)
Brother-in-law	Schwager (m)
brown	bruun
brown bread	dunkels Brot (n)
Brunch	Brunch (m)
Brush	Bürschtä (f)
Bug	Wanzä (f)
Building	Geboide (n)
Building (new)	Noibau (m)
Bull	Schtiär (m)
Bulletin board	Aschlagbrätt (n)
Bunker	Luftschuzzchäller (m)
burn (verb)	verbränä, görpsä, görpslä (Babys)
Bus	Bus (m)
Bus station	Busbaanhof (m)
Bus stop	Bushalteschtell (f)
Bus ticket	Busbilet (n)
Business casual	unzwungä
Butcher's shop	Mezzg (f)
Butter	Butter (m), Ankä (m)
Button	Chnopf (m)
buy (verb)	poschtä, chauffä
Buzzard	Moisebussard (m)
by (prep)	bi / bis
by (transp) (prep)	mit
Bye	Uf widerluägä, Uf widersee!, adieu (Adjö)
Bye (informal)	ciao (tschau), Tschüss

C

Cable TV	Kabelfernse (n)
Cake	Chuächa (m)
cancel (verb)	löschä, känslä
Candy	Zältli (n)
Canteen	Mensa (f), Kantinä (f)
Cap	Chappä (f)
Cappuccino	Cappuccino (m) (Gaputschino)
Car	Auto (n)
Care of	zuhandä vo
careful	Achtung
Carnival	Fasnacht (f)
Carpet	Teppich (m)
Carrots	Rüäbli (n)
Cash	Cash (Käsch), Bargäld (n)

Cash machine	Gäldautomat (m)
Cashier	Kassierer/in (m/f)
Cat	Chazz (f)
Cathedral	Katedraale (f)
Cauliflower	Bluämächöl (m)
Celebrity	Promi (m)
Celebrity	VIP (m) (Wiaipi)
Cellar	Chäller (m)
Century	Jaarhundert (n)
Chair	Schtuäl (m)
Chamois	Gäms (f)
Change (money)	Münz (n)
Channel	Kanal (m)
check in (verb)	iitschäggä
check out (verb)	uus-tschäggä
Cheek	Baggä (m)
cheerful	fröölich
Cheers	Proscht, Pröschtli
Cheese	Chäs (m)
Cheque	Schegg (m)
Cherry	Chriäsi (n)
Chest	Bruscht (f)
Chicken	Huän (n), Poulet (n) (Pule), Büsi (n)
Children's room	Chinderzimmer (n)
Chimney	Chämi (m)
Church	Chilä (f)
Cider	suurä Moscht (m)
Cigarette	Lungebröötli (n)(slang)
Cinema	Kino (n)
City	Schtadt(f), City (f) (Sitti)
City map	Schtadtplan (m)
Cleaner	Puzzma/frau (m/f)
Climate	Klima (n)
Clinic	Klinik (f)
Closet	Chaschtä (m)
Clothing	Chlaider (pl)
cloudy	wolkig, bedekkt
Coat	Mantel (m)
Cockroach	Kakerlakä (f)
Cocktail	Aperitif (m), Apero (m)
Code (secret)	Ghaimnummerä (f)
Code	Kod (m)
Coffee bar / cafe	Kafi (n)
Coffee break	Kafipausä (f)
Coffee party	Kafiklatsch (m), Kafichränzli (n)
Coffee with cream	Kafi (crème) (n)
Coffee with milk	Milchkafi (m) , Schalä (f)
Coin	Münzä (f)
Coke	Coggi (n)
Cold	Vercheltig (f)
cold	chalt
cold chocolate	chalti Schoggi (f)
cold drinks	chalti Getränk (pl)
Collar	Chragä (m)
Colleague	Arbetskolleg/in (m/f)
collect (verb)	sammlä

Comb	Schträäl (m)
comfortable	gediga (slang)
Commission	Komission (f)
complain (verb)	mozzä (slang)
Concert	Konzärt (m)
Concierge	Consierge (m) (Gonsiersch)
Concussion	Ghirnerschütterig (f)
Condiment	Aromat (m)
Condiment	Gwürz (pl)
Condom	Kondom (n)
Conference	Konfäränz (f)
Connection	Verbindig (f)
Consultant	Berater/in (m/f)
contagious	aschtekkänd
Continent	Kontinänt (m)
Contract	Vertrag (m)
Contraceptive	Verhüetigsmittel (n)
cool	cool (kuul)
cool (temperature)	chüel
copy (verb)	kopierä
Corn	Mais (m)
Corner	Eggä (m)
Corn on the cob	Mais-cholbä (m)
Costs	Choschtä (pl)
cosy	haimelig, gmüätlich
Cotton	Baumwule (f)
cough (verb)	huäschtä
Counter	Schalter (m)
Country	Land (n)
County	Kanton (m)
Course	Kurs (m)
Cousin	Cousine (f) (Gusinä), Cousin (m) (Gusän)
cover (verb)	zuähebä
Cow	Chuä (f)
Crab	Krabä (f)
Cramp	Chrampf (m)
crazy	verrukkt, gaga, irr
Cream	Raam (m), Crème (f) (Gräm)
Credit card	Kreditchartä (f)
Crocodile	Krokodil (n)
Croissant	Gipfeli (n)
Crossbow (shooting)	Armbruscht (schüssä)
Crossing	Chrüüzig (f)
cry (verb)	brüälä, hüülä
Culture	Kultur (f)
Cup	Tassä (f)
Curd cheese	Quark (m)
Currency	Wäärig (f)
Curtains	Vorhäng (pl)
Customer	Chund/in (m/f)
Customs	Zoll (m)
Cutlery	Pschtekk (n)

D

dance (verb)	tanzä
dark	dunkel

Dictionary

date (verb)	deitä	Driver's licence	Faaruuswis (m), Bi-let (n)	Family get-together	Familiäzämäkunft (f) , Familiäschluuch (m)
Daughter	Tochter (f)	Drops	Tröpfli (pl)	famous	berüämt / bekannt
Daughter-in-law	Schwigertochter (f)	drunk	blau (slang)	fantastic	fantastisch
Dawn	Dämmerig (f), Morgä-dämmerig (f)	dry	trochä	Farewell party	Apschidsfäscht (n)
Day	Tag (m)	dry out (verb)	uuströchnä	Fashion	Modä (f)
Debit card	EC-Chartä (f) (Eze-Chartä)	Dusk	Dämmerig (f), Aabig-dämmerig (f)	Father	Vatter (m)
Decade	Dekadä (f)	Duvet	Bettdekki (f)	Father -in-law	Schwigervatter (m)
December	Dezämber (m)			Faucet/ tap	Haanä (m)
declare (verb)	verzollä			February	Februar (m)
deep fried	frittiert	**E**		Fee	Gebür (f), Priis (m)
Deer	Hirsch (m)	Eagle	Adler (m)	Fever	Fiäber (n)
Delay	Verschpötig (f)	Ear	Oor (n)	few	wenig
Deli (katessen)	Delikatessladä (m)	early	früä	Fiancé	Verlobtä (m)
Deodorant	Deo (m)	earn money	Gäld verdiänä	Fiancée	Verlobti (f)
Department	Aptailig (f)	eat (verb)	biigä (slang)	Field	Fäld (n)
Departure	Abrais (f)	Editor	Herusgeber/in (m/f)	fifteen	füfzä
Deposit (money)	Depot (n) (Depo) , Hin-derlegig (f)	Egg	Ai (n)	fifth	füft
		Eggplant	Oberschinä (f)	fifty	füfzg
depressed	depressiv	eight	acht	Finger	Finger (m)
Desk	Pult (n)	eighteen	achzä	Fingernail	Fingernagel (m)
Desktop	Desktop (m)	eighth	acht	Fire	Füür (n)
desperate	verzwiiflet	eighty	achtzg	Fireplace	Cheminée (n) (Schminee)
Dessert	Dessert (m)	Elbow	Eläbogä (m)		
Detergent	Wöschmittel (n)	Electrical shop	Elektrogschäft (n)	first	erscht
Diabetes	Diabetis (f)	Elephant	Elefant (m)	First Aid	Erschti Hilf (f)
diabetic	diabetisch	eleven	elf	first floor	erschtä Schtokk
Diarrhoea	Durchfall (m)	Emergency	Notfall (m)	Fish	Fisch (m)
Diet	Diät (f)	Emergency room	Notufnaam (f)	fish (verb)	anglä, fischä
Digestive	Vertailer (m), Digestive (m) (Dischestiv)	emigrate (verb)	uusraisä	Fitness	Fitness
		Employee	Agschtellte (m), Agsch-tellti (f)	five	föif
Dining car	Schpiiswagä (m)			Flag	Faanä (f)
Dining room	Ässzimmer (n)	Employer	Arbetgeber/in (m/f)	Flavour	Gschmakk (m)
Dinner	Znacht (m), Znachtas-sä (n)	engaged	psezt	Floor	Bodä (m)
		engaged	verlobt	Flour	Määl (n)
Dinner service	Tischset (n)	Entertainment	Unterhaltig (f)	Flu	Grippe (f)
Director	Diräktor/in (m/f)	Entrance	ligang (m)	Fly	Flügä (f)
disappointed	enttüscht	Entry way	ligangshallä (f)	Foehn	Föön (m)
Discotheque	Disco (f)	Envelope	Couvert (n) (Kuwäär)	Fog	Näbel (m)
discount	reduziert	envious	niidisch	fold (verb)	faltä
Discounts	Verbilligung (f)	equals	isch glich, git	Foot	Fuäss (m)
Dishes	Gschirr (n)	Estate agency	Verwaltig (f)	Footpath	Wäg (m)
Dishwasher	Abwäschmaschine (f)	European ibex	Schtaibokk (m)	for (prep)	für
divorced	gschidä	even numbers	gradi Zaalä	Forecast	Wätterpricht (m)
Doctor	Arzt/(m) / Ärztin (f)	Evening	Aabig (m)	Forehead	Schtirn (f)
Doctor's surgery	Praxis (f)	Evening dress	Aabigchlaid (n)	Foreigner	Ussländer/in (m/f)
Dog	Hund (m)	Event	Event (m) (iwent), Aalass (m)	Forest	Wald (m)
Donkey	Esel (m)			Fork	Gablä (f)
Door	Tüür (f)	Exchange rate	Wächselratä (f)	Form	Formular (n)
Doorbell	Huusgloggä (f)	excited	uufgreggt	forty	vierzg
Double bed	Doppelbett (n)	Excuse me	entschuldigung, exgüsi	forward (verb)	forwardä, wiiterlaitä
down	abä	expensive	tüür	four	vier
Draft beer	Schtangä (f)	Exposition	Uus-schtellig (f)	fourteen	vierzä
Drawer	Schubladä (f)	Expresso	Espresso (m)	fourth	viert
Dress (noun)	Chlaid (n)	Eye	Aug (n)	Fox	Fuchs (m)
dress (verb)	aaziiä	Eyebrow	Augebrauä (f)	Freckles	Märzetüpfli (pl)
Dress code	Chlaidervorschrift (f)	Eyelash	Wimperä (pl)	Freezer	Tüfchüäler (m)
dressed	aazogä			fresh	früsch
Dressing	Salatsossä (f)	**F**		Friday	Friitig
		Face	Gsicht (n)	Fridge	Chüälschrank (m)

Dictionary

fried	prötlet	Hail	Hagel (m)	in (prep)	in
Friend	Fründ/in (m/f)	hail (verb)	haglä	in front of (prep)	vor
from (prep)	us, vo	Hair	Haar (pl)	Income	Iikomä (n)
Frontier	Gränzä (f)	halal	halal	Infection	Enzündig (f)
frozen	tüfgfrorä	Half board	Halbpension (f)	Injection	Schprüzzä (f)
Fruit	Frucht (f)	Hallway	Gang (m)	Injury	Verlezzig (f)
Frying pan	Bratpfanä (f)	Ham	Schinkä (m)	Insect	Insekt (n)
Full board	Vollpension (f)	Hand	Hand (f)	Insomnia	Schlaflosikait (f)
Full time	vollziit	Hand cream	Handcreme (f) (Hand-	Insurance	Versicherig (f)
funny	luschtig, wizzig		gräm)	Insurance number	Versicherigsnumme-
furious	hässig	Hand dryer	Händtröchner (m)		rä (f)
Future	Zuäkumft (f) , zu-	Hanger	Chlaiderbügel (m)	Intensive care	Intensivschtazion (f)
	äkümftig	happy	glükklich	Interest	Zins (m)
		Hat	Huät (m)	International	Ussland-Nachrichtä (pl)
		Hay fever	Hoischnuppä (m)	news	

G		Head	Chopf (m)	into (prep)	gägä, in
gamble (verb)	schpilä, gämblä	Headache	Chopfwee (n)	invest money	Gäld inweschtierä
Game	Schpiil (n)	Headlines	Schlagzilä (pl)	Investment	Inweschtizion (f), In-
Garage	Garage (f) (Garasch)	hear (verb)	ghörä		weschtierig (f)
Garden	Gartä (m)	Heart	Härz (n)	Invoice	Rächnig (f)
Garlic	Chnobli (m), Chno-	Heat	Hizz (f)	Iron	Bügälisä (n)
	blauch (m)	Hello	Grüezi	Island	Inslä (f)
gay	schwul	Help	Hilfe (f)		
Geography	Geografii (f)	Hen night	Polteraabig (m)	**J**	
Girl	Maitli (n)	here	da		
Glass	Glas (n)	heterosexual	hetero(sexuell)	Jack salmon	Zander (m)
Gloves	Häntschä (pl)	Hi (informal)	Hoi, Sali, Salü	Jackdaw	Doolä (f)
Goat	Gaiss (f)	Hi (to several)	Hoi zäme	Jacket	Jagge (f)
gold (colour)	gold	Highway	Autobaan (f)	Jam	Gomfi (f)
good	guet	Hill	Hügel (m)	Jam doughnut	Berliner (m)
Goose bumps	Huänerhuut (f)	Hip	Hüft (f)	January	Januar (m)
Gossip	Klatsch (m), Tratsch	Hippopotamus	Flusspferd (n), Nil-	jealous	ifersüchtig
	(m)		pferd (n)	Jeans	Jeans (pl) (Tschins)
gossip (verb)	klatschä	hold (verb)	hebä	Job application	Bewärbig (f)
grab (verb)	griiffä, feschthebä	homosexual	homo(sexuell)	Job description	Jobbeschribig (f)
Grandchild	Gros-chind (n)	Honey	Honig (m)	Job interview	Bewärbigsgs-
Granddaughter	Änkelin (f)	horny	schpizz, giggerig		chpräch(n)
Grandfather	Grosvatter (m)	Horse	Ross (n)	Joke	Wizz (m)
Grandmother	Grosmuetter (f)	Hospital	Schpital (n)	joyful	froo
Grandparents	Groselterä (pl)	hot	haiss	joyful	zfridä
Grandson	Änkel (m)	hot chocolate	haissi Schoggi (f)	Juice	Saft (m)
Grapefruit juice	Grapefruitsaft (m)	hot milk	haissi Milch (f)	July	Juli (m)
	(Gräpfrüsaft)	hot wine	Glüäwii (m)	jump (verb)	gumpä
Grape juice	Truubesaft (m)	Hour	Schtund (f)	June	Juni (m)
grateful	dankbar	House number	Huusnummerä (f)	**K**	
Great aunt	Grostantä (f)	Housewarming	Husiweiigs-party (f)		
Great grandfather	Urgrosvatter (m)	How?	Wiä?	Key	Schlüssel (m)
Great grand-	Urgrosmuetter (f)	hug (verb)	umarmä	kiss (verb)	küssä
mother		humid	füecht	Kitchen	Chuchi (f)
Great uncle	Grosunggle (m)	Humour	Humoor (m)	Kitchen shelves	Chuchiablagä (pl)
green	grüän	hundred	hundert	Knee	Chnü (n)
grey	grau	hungry	Hunger (m)	Knife	Mässer (n)
Grill	Grill (m)	hurry	schnäll	kosher	koscher
grilled	griliert	Husband	Maa (m)	**L**	
Groceries	Läbesmittel (pl)				
Ground floor	Partär (n)	**I**		Laboratory	Labor (n)
Guinea pig	Meersoili (n)			Lake	See (m)
Gutters	Tachrinnä (f)	Ice cream	Glacé (n) (Glasse)	Lamb	Lamm (n)
Gym	Fitnessruum (m)	Iced tea	Iis-tee (m)	land (verb)	landä
H		Idiot	Mönggi (n) (slang)	Landlord	Vermieter/in (m/f)
		immigrate (verb)	iiraisä	Laptop	Laptop (m) (Läptop)

Dictionary

large	gross					
late	schpaat					
Latte Macchiato	Latte Macchiato (f) (Maggiato)					
laugh (verb)	lachä					
Laundry	Wösch (f)					
Laundry bag	Wöschsakk (m)					
Laundry basket	Zaine (f)					
Laundry day	Wöschtag (m)					
Laundry room	Wöschchuchi (f)					
Laundry schedule	Wöschplan (m)					
Lawn	Rasä (m)					
Lawnmower	Rasämäier (m)					
Leather	Läder (n)					
leave (verb)	abfaarä					
left	linggs					
Leg	Bai (n)					
Legumes	Hülsäfrücht (pl)					
Lemon	Zitrone (f)					
Lentils	Linsä (pl)					
lesbian	lesbisch					
less	weniger					
Letter	Briäf (m)					
Lettuce	Chopfsalat (m)					
Library	Bibliothek (f)					
lick (verb)	lutschä					
Lift	Lift (m)					
light (colour)	hell					
Lightning	Blizz (m)					
Lilac	lila					
Lime	Limone (f)					
Linen	Liinä (f)					
Lion	Loi (m)					
listen (verb)	losä					
Liver	Läbere (f)					
Lizard	Aidächsli (n)					
Loan	Darleä (n)					
Lobby	Vorhallä (f), Vorruum (m)					
Lobster	Hummer (m)					
Local call	lokale Aaruäf (m)					
Local news	lokali Noiigkaitä (pl), lokali Nachrichtä (pl)					
log in (verb)	iiloggä					
log out (verb)	uusloggä					
lonely	ainsam					
long	lang					
long distance call	internazionalä, Aaruäf (m)					
long sleeves	langärmlig					
long-sighted	wiitsichtig					
look (verb)	luägä					
Loss	Verluscht (m)					
Lounge	Schtubä (f)					
love (verb)	liäbä					
lovely	härzig					
lucky number	Glükkszaal (f)					
Luggage	Gepäkk (n)					
Lunch	Zmittagässä (n), Zmittag (m)					

Lunch break	Mittagspausä (f)
Lynx	Luchs (m)

M

Magazine	Heftli (n)
Magic	Zauberai (f)
magic, to do (verb)	zaubärä
Mailbox	Briäfchaschtä (m)
Main course	Hauptschpiis (f)
Make-up	Schminkzüg (n)
Manager	Manager/in (m/f) (Mänätscher/in)
many	vill
Map	Chartä (f)
March	März (m)
Margarine	Margerinä (f)
marinated	mariniert
Marital status	Familiäschtand (m)
Marmalade	Orangschägomfi (f)
Marmot	Murmeli (n), Mumeltiär (n)
Marriage	Ehe (f)
married	verhüratet
Marten	Marder (m)
Massage	Massage (f) (Masaasch)
May	Mai (m)
Meals	Maalzitä (pl)
Meat	Flaisch (n)
Medicine	Hailmittel (n)
medium (size)	mittleri Grössi, äs M
medium (meat)	halb durä
Meeting	Beschprächig (f), Sizzig (f)
Microwave	Mikrowälä (f)
mild	mild
Milk	Milch (f)
milk (verb)	mälchä
Millennium	Jaartuusig (n)
million	Million (f)
Mineral water	Mineralwasser (n)
minus	minus
Minute	Minutä (f)
Minutes	Protokoll (n)
Mirror	Schpiägel (m)
Mobile phone	Händi(n)
Mobile phone	Natel (n)
moment	Momänt (m)
Monday	Mäntig
Money	Gäld (n)
Monkey	Aff (m)
Month	Monät (m)
more	mee
Morning	Morgä (m)
Mosque	Moschee (f)
Mosquito	Muggä (f)
Mother	Muetter (f)
Mother-in-law	Schwigermuetter (f)
Mountain	Bärg (m)

Mouse	Muus (f), Müsli (n)
Mouth	Muul (n)
move out (verb)	uusziä
much	vill
Museum	Museum (n)
Music	Musig (f)

N

Nail	Nagel (m)
Napkin	Serviettä (f)
National news	Inland-Nachrichtä (pl)
Neck	Nakkä (f)
Neighbours	Nachbarä (pl)
Nephew	Näffä (m)
news	Nachrichtä (pl)
Newspaper	Zitig (f)
next to (prep)	näbäd
Niece	Nichtä (f)
Night	Nacht (f)
nine	nün
nineteen	nünzä
ninety	nünzg
ninth	nünt
Nipple	Bruschtwarzä (f)
no	nai
Noon/ midday	Mittag (m)
Nose	Nasä (f)
nothing	nüt
November	Novämber (m)
now	jezt
Nurse	Chrankäschwöschter (f)
Nurse	Pflägfachfrau/maa (f/m)
Nylon	Nylon (n) (Nailon)

O

Obituary	Todesaazaig (f)
Occupation	Job (m) (Tschop)
Occupation	Pruäf (m)
Ocean	Ozean (m)
October	Oktober (m)
odd numbers	ungradi Zaalä
of (prep)	vo
Office	Gschäft (n)
Office	Büro (n)
old building	Altbau (m)
old man	altä Maa
old woman	alti Frau
Olive oil	Olivenöl (n)
on (hor. surfaces)	uf
on (ver. surfaces)	a(m)
one	äis
one thousand	(ain)-tuusig
One-room apt.	Aizimmerwonig (f)
Onion	Zwiblä (f)
Onion	Bölä (pl)
Opera	Operä (f)
Operation	Operazion (f)
Operator	Vermittlig (f)

Opinion	Mainig (f)	Plate	Täller (m)
opposite (prep)	gägänüber	Platform	Perron (n)
orange (colour)	orangsch	play (verb)	geimä, schpilä
Orange	Orangschä (f)	play football (verb)	tschutä
Orange juice	Orangschäsaft (m), O-Saft (m)	please	bitte
order (verb)	pschtelä	Plug	Schtekker (m)
Oven	Ofä (m)	plus	plus
over (prep)	über	plus (maths)	und
Overtime	Überschtundä (pl)	Poison	Gift (n)
Owner	Psizzer/in (m/f)	poisoned	vergiftet

P

		Polyester	Polyester (m), (Polijeschter)
Packet	Päkkli (n)	Pork	Schwinigs (n), Schwaineflaisch (n)
Pain	Schmärzä (pl)		
Pain Killer	Schmärzmittel (n)	Post	Poscht (f)
Painful	schmärzhaft	Post office	Poscht (f)
Pan	Pfanä (f)	Postage stamp	Poschtschtämpfel (m)
Panties	Underhosä (f)	Postal money order	Gäldüberwiisig (f)
Paper towel	Papiertuäch (n)		
Parasite	Parasit (m)	Postcard	Poschtchartä (f)
Parent's home	Elterähuus (n)	Postcode	Poschtlaitzaal (f)
Park	Park (m)	Postman	Pöschtler/in (m/f)
Parking area	Parkplazz (m)	Potatoes	Herdöpfel (m)
Part time	tailziit	Prawns	Riisecrevettä (f) (Riisägröwettä)
Partner	Partner/in (m/f)		
Partner (love)	Läbäs-Partner/in (m/f)	pray (verb)	bätä
Party	Party (f) (Parti), Fäscht (n)	Prescription	Rezäpt (n)
		present	jezt
Passenger	Passaschiir (m)	Present	Gägäwart (f)
Passport	Pass (m)	Presentation	Präsentazion (f)
past	vergangä	press (verb)	drukkä
Past	Vergangähait (f)	Price	Priis (m)
Pasta	Pasta (f) , Taigwarä (pl)	Professional	Profi (m)
Pastry	Gebäkk (n)	Profit	Profit (m)
Path	Wäg (m)	Public telephone	öffentlichs Telefon (n)
Patient	Paziänt/in (m/f)	Punch	Punsch (m)
pay (verb)	zalä	Purchase order	Pschtellig (f), Uuftrag (m)
Payment	Zalig (f)		
peaceful	fridlich (slang)	Purse	Handtäschli (n)
Peak	Gipfel (m)		
Peanut butter	Erdnussbutter (m)		
Pear	Birä (f)		

R

Penis	Penis (m)	Rabbit	Chüngel (m)
Pension fund	Pensionskassä (f)	Rabies	Tollwuät (f)
Pension number	Ahavau-Nummerä (f)	Radio	Radio (m)
Pepper	Pepperoni (f)	Rain	Räge (m)
Perch	Egli (m), Barsch (m)	Rappen	Rappä (m)
Permit	Bewilligung (f), Genemigung (f)	rare	bluetig
		Raspberry	Himbeeri (n)
Petrol	Bänzin (n)	raw	roo
Petrol station	Tankschtell (f)	Razor blades	Rasiärklingä (f)
Phone call	Aaruäf (m)	read (verb)	läsä
Phone number	Telefonnummerä (f)	Reception	Empfang (m), Rezepzion (f)
Photo	Foti (n)		
Pie	Wäjä (f)	Receptionist	Resepzionischt/in (m/f)
Pig	Sau (f)		
Pike	Hecht (m)	red	rot
Pillow	Chüssi (n)	Red wine	Rotwii (m) / Rotä (m)
pink	rosa	Registered letter	igschribnä Briäf (m)
Plan	Plan (m)	Relatives	Verwandti (pl)
Plane ticket	Flugzüg-Tikket (n)	Remote control	Fernbediänig (f)
		Rental flat	Mietwonig (f)

reply (verb)	antwortä, zruggschriibä
Report	Pricht (m)
reserve (verb)	reserviärä
Residence permit	Ufenthaltsgenemigung (f)
Restaurant	Reschtorant (m), Baiz (f)
Rhinoceros	Nashorn (n)
Rice	Riis (m)
right	rächts
River	Fluss (m)
roasted	gröschtet
Roe	Ree (n)
Roll	Brötli (n), Pürli (n)
Roof	Tach (n)
Room	Zimmer (n)
Room service	Zimmerservice (m) (Zimmer-Serwis)
Rooster	Güggel (m)
Rubbish bin	Apfall(chübel) (m)
Rucksack	Rukksakk (m)

S

sad	truurig
Salad	Salat (m)
Salami	Salami (m)
Salary	Loon (m), Salär (n)
Sale (rebate)	Uusverchauff
Salesperson	Verchoiffer/in (m/f)
Salmon	Lachs (m)
salty	salzig
Sandwich	Sandwich (m) (Sändwitsch)
Satellite	Satellit (m)
Satellite Dish	Satellitäschüsslä (f)
Saturday	Samschtig
Sausage	Wurscht (f)
save (verb)	schparä
Savings account	Schparkonto (n)
Scales	Waag (f)
Scarf	Schal (m), Tuäch (n)
School	Schuäl (f)
Sea	Meer (n)
Seafood	Meeresfrücht (pl)
Season	Jaaresziit (f)
second	zwait
Second (time)	Sekundä (f)
Secretary	Sekretär/in (m/f)
Section	Apschnitt (m), Tail (m)
Security	Sicherhait (f)
see (verb)	gsee
sell (verb)	verchauffä
send (verb)	sändä, schikkä
Sender's address	Apsänder/in (m/f)
sentimental	sentimental
separate (verb)	sich tränä
separated	trännt
September	Septämber (m)
Service area	Raschtplazz (m), Raschtschtettä (f)
seven	sibä

seventeen	sibzä
seventh	sibät
seventy	sibäzg
sexy	sexy
shake (verb)	schüttlä
Shame, what a	Schad!
Shampoo	Schampoo (n)
Sheet	Bettuäch (n)
Shirt	Hämp (n)
Shoes	Schuä (pl)
Shop	Ladä (m)
shop (verb)	iichauffä
shopping (go)	lädälä
Shopping bag	iichaufs-Täschä (f)
Shopping centre	Ichaufszentrum (n)
short	churz
short sleeves	churzärmlig
Shorts	Shorts (pl)
short-sighted	churzsichtig
Shoulder	Schulterä (f)
Shower	Duschi (f)
Shower cream	Duschmittel (n)
Shower curtain	Duschvorhang (m)
Shrimp	Crevettä (f) (Gröwettä)
shy	schüch
Siblings	Gschwüschterti (pl)
sick	chrank
Signature	Unterschrift (f)
Silk	Sidä (f)
silver (colour)	silber
single	ledig, single
Sister	Schwö(schter) (f)
Sister-in-law	Schwögerin (f)
six	sächs
sixteen	sächzä
sixth	sächst
sixty	sächzg
Skin	Huut (f)
Skirt	Rokk (m), Jupe (m) (Schüpp)
Slug	Schnägg (m)
sleepy	müäd, schlapp, schlöfrig
Slippers	Finkä (pl)
small	chlii
smell	schmökkä
smile	lächlä
Smoking area	Rauchereggä (m)
Snack (afternoon)	Zvieri (m)
Snack (morning)	Znüni (m)
Snake	Schlangä (f)
Snow	Schnee (m)
Soap	Soiffä (f)
Society	Gsellschaft (f)
Socks	Sokkä (pl)
Soft drink	Blöterliwasser (n)
some	äs paar, ainigi
somebody	öpper
somehow	irgendwiä
something	öppis

sometimes	mängisch
somewhere	noimät
Son	Soon (m)
Son-in-law	Schwigersoon (m)
soon	bald
sorry	sorry
so-so	so so (la la)
sour	suur
Space	Ruum (m)
speak (verb)	redä
Speed camera	Radar (m)
Speed limit	Gschwindigkaitsbe-gränzig (f)
spend (verb)	uusgä
spicy	scharf
Spider	Schpinä (f)
Spinach	Schpinat (m)
Spirit	Schnaps (m)
Spoon	Löffel (m)
Sports	Schport (m)
Spring	Früälig (m)
Stairs	Schtägä (f)
Stamp	Markä (f)
stare (verb)	schtarrä
Starter	Vorschpiis (f)
State	Schtaat (m)
Steak	Steak (n) (Steik)
Stockings	Schtrümpf (pl)
Stomach	Magä (m)
Stomachache	Buuchwee (n)
Store	Ladä (m)
Storm	Schturm (m)
Stove	Härd (m)
straight on	graduus
Strawberry	Erdbeeri (n)
Street	Schtrass (f)
stressed	gschtresst
Studio	Schtudio (n)
stupid	blööd, doof
Subject	Thema (n)
suck (verb)	sugä
Sugar	Zukker (m)
Suit (for man)	Aazug (m)
Suit (for woman)	Koschtüm (n)
Summer	Summer (m)
Sun	Sunä (f)
Sunday	Sunntig
sunny	sunig
Sunshade	Sunätach (n)
super	hammer (slang), mega (slang)
Supermarket	Supermärt (m)
surprised	überrascht
sweet	süäss
sweetie	Schnugi
swim (verb)	schwümä
Swimming pool	Schwümmbad (n)
Swiss accordion	Handörgeli (n)
Swiss Francs	Schwiizer Frankä (m)
Swiss wrestling	schwingä

Synagogue	Synagogä (f)

T

Table	Tisch (m)
Table cloth	Tischtuäch (n)
Table mats	Tischmattä (f)
Take away	Take away (m) , (Teik Awei)
Talk show	Talk Show (f), (Tok Schou)
Tangerine	Mandarinli (n)
tasteless	fad, gschmakklos
Taxes	Schtürä (pl)
Tea	Tee (m)
Teaspoon	Teelöffeli (n)
Technician	Techniker/in (m/f)
Teenager	Teeni (m) (Tiini)
telephone (verb)	aalütä
Telephone bill	Telefonrächnig (f)
Telephone book	Telefonbuäch (n)
Telephone card	Telefonchartä (f)
Television	Fernse (n)
Television licence	Fernsebewilligung (f)
Temperature	Temperatur (f)
ten	zä
Tenant	Mieter/in (m/f)
Tennis Shoes	Tennisschuä (pl)
tenth	zät
Terrace	Terrassä (f)
Text message	SMS (n) (Äsämäs)
thank you	danke, merci (märsi)
thousand	tuusig
Theatre	Theater (n)
there	deet
Thief	Diäb (m)
thing	Sach (f) , Ding (n)
third	dritt
thirsty	Durscht (m)
thirteen	drizä
thirty	drissg
three	drü
Throat	Hals (m)
through (prep)	dur(ch)
Thunder	Dunner (m)
Thunderstorm	Gwitter (n)
Thursday	Dunnschtig
Tie	Grawattä (f)
Tiger	Tiger (m)
to (prep)	zu
Toast	Tooscht (m)
Today	hüt
Toe	Zäjä (m)
Toenail	Zäjänagel (m)
Toilet	Toilettä (f) (Tualettä)
Toilet	WC (n) (Weze)
Toiletry bag	Necessaire (n) (Nes-sessär)
Toilet paper	WC-Papier (n) , (Weze-Papier)
Toiletries	Badzimmersachä (pl)

Tomato	Tomatä (f)
Tomorrow	morn
Tongue	Zungä (f)
Tooth	Zaa (m)
Toothbrush	Zaabürschteli (n)
Toothpaste	Zaapaschtä (f)
Top	Obertail (n)
Top floor	oberschti Schtokk (m)
touch (verb)	berüärä, aalangä
Tourist	Turischt/in (m/f), Turi (m) (slang)
Towel	Tüächli (n)
Town	Schtadt (f)
Track	Glais (n)
Traffic light	Amplä (f)
Train	Zug (m)
Train station	Baanhof (m)
Train ticket	Zugbilet (n)
Trainee	Praktikant/in (m/f)
transfer (verb)	überwiisä
Trash	Apfallchorb (m)
Travellers' cheque	Traveller cheques (pl) (Träwälär Schegg)
Tree	Baum (m)
Trousers	Hosä (f)
Trout	Forälä (f)
T-Shirt	T-Shirt (n), Liibli (n)
Tuesday	Ziischtig
Tumble drier	Tumbler (m)(Tömbler)
Tuna	Ton (m)
Turkey	Truthaan (m)
Turtle	Schildchrot (f)
twelve	zwölf
twenty	zwänzg
Twins	Zwilling (pl)
two	zwai
two hundred	zwaihundert
two thousand	zwaituusig
Two-room apt.	Zwaizimmerwonig(f)

U

Uncle	Unggle (m)
under (prep)	under
Underwear	Underwösch (f)
Uniform	Uniform (f)
Unlucky number	Ungl ükkszaal (f)
until (prep)	bis
Up	ufä
Urinal	Pissoir (n) (Pissuar)
Utility room	Apschtellruum (m)

V

vacant	frei
Vacations	Feriä (pl)
Vagina	Vagina (f)
Valley	Taal (n)
Veal	Chalbflaisch (n)
vegan	vegan(isch)
Vegetables	Gmüäs (n)
vegetarian	vegetarisch
vigorous	energisch
Village	Dörfli (n)
Vinegar	Essig (m)
violet	violett
Virus	Wirus (m)
Visa	Wisum (n)

W

Waist	Talliä (f)
Wake up call	Wekkaaruäf (m)
Ward	Schtazion(f)
Ward	Aptailig (f) (f)
Wardrobe	Gardäröbä (f)
Warehouse	Lagerhallä (f), Warähuus (n)
warm	warm
Washbasin	Brüneli (n), Lavabo (n)
wash (verb)	wäschä
Washing machine	Wöschmaschine (f)
Wasp	Wäschpi (n)
watch (verb)	luägä
Water with gas	Wasser mit Cholesüüri
Water without gas	Wasser ooni Cholesüüri
Watermelon	Wassermelonä (f)
Weather	Wätter (n)
Weather report	Wätterpricht (m)
Wedding	Hochziit (f)
Wedding eve's party	Polteraabig (m)
Wednesday	Mittwuch
Week	Wuchä (f)
Weekend	Wuchänänd (n)
Welcome	Willkomä
What ?	Was ?
When?	Wänn?
Where to?	Wohi?
Where?	Wo?
whisper (verb)	flüschterä
white	wiiss
White bread	Wiissbrot (n)
White fish	Felchä (f)
White wine	Wiisswii (m), Wiissä (m)

Who?	Wär?
Whole grain bread	Vollkornbrot (n)
Why?	Warum?
wide	wiit
Widow	Witwe (f)
widowed	verwitwet
Widower	Witwer (m)
Wife	Frau (f)
wiggle (verb)	gwagglä
Wild boar	Wildsau (f)
Wind	Wind (m)
Wind surfing	Wind sörfä
Window	Fänschter (n)
Wine	Wii (m)
wink (verb)	zwinkerä
Winter	Winter (m)
with (prep)	mit
withdraw (verb)	abhebä
without	ooni
Wolf	Wolf (m)
Wool	Wulä (f)
Worker	Arbaiter/in (m/f)
World	Wält (f)
Worm	Wurm (m)
worried	besorgt

Y

yawn (verb)	gäänä
Year	Jaar (n)
yellow	gääl
yes	ja
Yesterday	geschter
yodel (verb)	jodlä
Yoghurt	Joghurt (n) (Jogurt)
young man	Purscht (m), jungä Maa (m)
young woman	jungi Frau (f) , Frölain (n)

Z

Zebra	Zebra (n)
zero	null
Zoo	Zoo (m)

THIS WAY TO THE
SWISS GERMAN TO ENGLISH DICTIONARY

Dictionary

Swiss German – English

A

a	at (prep)
a(m)	on (prep)
Aabig (m)	Evening
Aabigchlaid (n)	Evening dress
Aabigdämmerig (f)	Dusk
aalangä	touch (verb)
Aalass (m)	Event
aalütä	telephone (verb)
Aaruäf (m)	Phone call
aaziiä	dress (verb)
aazogä	dressed
Aazug (m)	Suit
abä	down
abfaarä	leave (verb)
abhebä	withdraw (verb)
Abrais (f)	Departure
Abwäschmaschine(f)	Dishwasher
acht	eight
acht	eighth
Achtung	careful
achtzg	eighty
achzä	eighteen
Addrässbüäch (n)	Address book
adieu (adjö)	Bye
Adler (m)	Eagle
Adrässä (f)	Address
Aff (m)	Monkey
Agschtellte (m)	Employee
Agschtellti (f)	Employee
Ahavau-Nummerä(f)	Pension number
Ai (n)	Egg
Aidächsli (n)	Lizard
ainigi	some
ainsam	lonely
äis	one
(ain)-tuusig	one thousand
Aizimmerwonig (f)	One-room apt.
Akunft (f)	Arrival
Alergii (f)	Allergy
alergisch gägä	allergic to
Alphorn (m)	Alpenhorn
altä Maa	old man
Altbau (m)	old building
alti Frau	old woman
Amaisä (f)	Ant

Ambulanz (f)	Ambulance
Amplä (f)	Traffic light
anglä	fish (verb)
ängschtlich	afraid , anxious
Ankä (m)	Butter
Änkel (m)	Grandson
Änkelin (f)	Granddaughter
antwortä	reply (verb)
Aperitif (m)	Cocktail
Apero (m)	Cocktail
Apfallchorb (m)	Trash
Apfallchübel (m)	Rubbish bin
April (m)	April
Apsänder/in (m/f)	Sender's address
Apschidsfäscht (n)	Farewell party
Apschnitt (m)	Section
Apschtellruum (m)	Utility room
Apszäss (m)	Abscess
Aptailig (f)	Ward, Department
Arbaiter/in	Worker
Arbetgeber/in (m/f)	Employer
Arbetskolleg/in (m/f)	Colleague
Arbetsmappä (f)	Briefcase
Arm (m)	Arm
Armbruscht (schüssä)	Crossbow (shooting)
Aromat (n)	Condiment
Artikel (m)	Article
Arzt (m)	Doctor
Ärztin (f)	Doctor
äs paar	some
Aschlagbrätt (n)	Bulletin board
Aschpirin (n)	Aspirin
aschtekkänd	contagious
Aschtma (n)	Asthma
Asischtänt/in (m/f)	Assistant
Ässzimmer (n)	Dining room
Attachment (n) (Attäts-chmänt)	Attachment
Attikawonig (f)	Attic flat
Aug (n)	Eye
Augebrauä (f)	Eyebrow
Auguscht (m)	August
Auto (n)	Car
Autobaan (f)	Highway

B

B&B (n)	B&B

Baanhof (m)	Train station
Badwannä (f)	Bath tub
Badzimmer (n)	Bathroom
Badzimmersachä (pl)	Toiletries
Baggä (m)	Cheek
Bai (n)	Leg
Baiz (f)	Restaurant
bald	soon
Balkon (m)	Balcony
Bananä (f)	Banana
Bank (f)	Bank
Bankkonto (n)	Bank account
Banknotä (f)	Banknotes
Bänzin (n)	Petrol
Bar (f)	Bar
Bär (m)	Bear
Bärg (m)	Mountain
Bargäld (n)	Cash
Barsch (m)	Perch
bätä	pray (verb)
Baum (m)	Tree
Baumwule (f)	Cotton
bedekkt	cloudy
Beha (m)	Bra
beige (bäsch)	beige
Bekk (m)	Bakery
Bekkerei (f)	Bakery
Berater/in (m/f)	Consultant
Berliner (m)	Jam doughnut
berüämt / bekannt	famous
berüärä	touch (verb)
Beschprächig (f)	Meeting
besorgt	worried
Bett (n)	Bed
Bettaazug (m)	Bed cover
Bettdekki (f)	Duvet
Bettuäch (n)	Sheet
Bewärbig (f)	Job application
Bewärbigsgschpräch(n)	Job interview
Bewilligung (f)	Permit
bi	at (prep), by (prep)
Biändli (n)	Bee
Biär (n)	Beer
Bibliothek (f)	Library
biigä (slang)	eat (verb)
Biinä (f)	Bee
Bilet (n)	Driver's licence

Birä (f)	Pear	Cash (Käsch)	Cash	Cousine (f) (Gusinä)	Cousin
bis	by (prep), until (prep)	Chäfer (m)	Beetle	Couvert (n) (Kuwäär)	Envelope
bitte	please	Chalbflaisch (n)	Veal	Crème (f) (Gräm)	Cream
bitter	bitter	Challer (m)	Cellar	Crevettä (f) (Gröwettä)	Shrimp
blasä	blow (verb)	chalt	cold		

D

blau	blue	Chalti Getränk (pl)	cold drinks	da	here
blau (slang)	drunk	Chalti Schoggi (f)	cold chocolate	Dämmerig (f)	Dawn, Dusk
Blinddarmenzündig (f)	Appendicitis	Chämi (n)	Chimney	dankbar	grateful
blinzlä	blink (verb)	Chappä (f)	Cap	danke	thank you
Blizz (m)	Lightning	Chartä (f)	Map	Darleä (n)	Loan
blööd	stupid	Chäs (m)	Cheese	deet	there
Blöterliwasser (n)	Soft drink	Chaschtä (f)	Closet	deitä	date (verb)
Bluämächöl (m)	Cauliflower	chauffä	buy (verb)	Dekadä (f)	Decade
Bluät (n)	Blood	Chazz (f)	Cat	Delikatessladä (m)	Deli(katessen)
Bluätdrukk (m)	Blood pressure	Chef/in (m/f) (Schef/in)	Boss	Deo (m)	Deodorant
Bluätzukker (m)	Blood sugar	Cheminée(n)(Schminee)	Fireplace	Depot (n) (Depo)	Deposit (money)
bluetig	rare	Chilä (f)	Church	depressiv	depressed
Blusä (f)	Blouse	Chinderzimmer (n)	Children's room	Desktop (m)	Desktop
Bodä (m)	Floor	Chischtä (f)	Box	Dessert (m)	Dessert
Bölä (pl)	Onion	Chlaid (n)	Dress (noun)	Dezämber (m)	December
Bonus (m)	Bonus	Chlaider (pl)	Clothing	Diäb (m)	Thief
Boonä (f)	Beans	Chlaiderbügel (m)	Hanger	Diabetis (f)	Diabetes
bös	angry	Chlaidervorschrift (f)	Dress code	diabetisch	diabetic
Bratpfanä (f)	Frying pan	chlii	small	Diät (f)	Diet
Briäf (m)	Letter	Chnoblauch (m)	Garlic	Digestive (m) (Dischestiv)	Digestive
Briäfchaschtä (m)	Mailbox	Chnobli (m)	Garlic		
Broggoli (m)	Broccoli	Chnochäbruch (m)	Broken bone	Ding (n)	Thing
Brot (n)	Bread	Chnöchel (m)	Ankle	Diräktor/in (m/f)	Director
Brötli (n)	Roll	Chnopf (m)	Button	Disco (f)	Discotheque
Brüäder (m)	Brother	Chnü (n)	Knee	doof	stupid
brüälä	cry (verb)	Chopf (m)	Head	Doolä (f)	Jackdaw
Brugg (f)	Bridge	Chopfsalat (m)	Lettuce	Doppelbett (n)	Double bed
Brunch (m)	Brunch	Chopfwee (n)	Headache	Dörfli (n)	Village
Brüneli (n)	Washbasin	Choschtä (pl)	Costs	drissg	thirty
Bruscht (f)	Chest	Chragä (m)	Collar	dritt	third
Bruschtwarzä (f)	Nipple	Chrampf (m)	Cramp	drizä	thirteen
bruun	brown	chrank	sick	drü	three
Buäb (m)	Boy	Chrankäschwöschter (f)	Nurse	drukkä	press (verb)
Büäbli (n)	Baby boy	Chrankäwagä (m)	Ambulance	dunkel	dark
Buäch (n)	Book	Chriäsi (n)	Cherry	dunkels Brot (n)	brown bread
Büächergschtell (n)	Book shelves	Chrüüzig (f)	Crossing	Dunner (m)	Thunder
Büächerladä (m)	Bookshop	Chuä (f)	Cow	Dunnschtig	Thursday
Buächhandlig (f)	Bookshop	Chuächä (m)	Cake	dur(ch)	through (prep)
Buchnabel (m)	Bellybutton	Chüälschrank (m)	Fridge	Durchfall (m)	Diarrhoea
Bügälisä (n)	Iron	Chuchi (f)	Kitchen	Durscht (m)	Thirsty
Büro (n)	Office	Chuchiablagä (pl)	Kitchen shelves	Duschi (f)	Shower
Bürschtä (f)	Brush	chüel	cool (temperat.)	Duschmittel (n)	Shower cream
Bus (m)	Bus	Chund/in (m/f)	Customer	Duschvorhang (m)	Shower curtain
Busä (m)	Breast	Chüngel (m)	Rabbit		

E

Busbaanhof (m)	Bus station	churz	short	EC-Chartä (f) (Eze-Chartä)	Debit card
Busbilet (n)	Bus ticket	churzärmlig	short sleeves		
Bushalteschtell (f)	Bus stop	churzsichtig	short-sighted	Eggä (m)	Corner
Büsi (n)	Cat	Chüssi (n)	Pillow	Egli (m)	Perch
Butter (m)	Butter	ciao (tschau)	Bye (informal)	Ehe (f)	Marriage
Buuch (m)	Abdomen	City (f) (Sitti)	City	Eläbogä (m)	Elbow
Buuchwee (n)	Stomachache	Coggi (n)	Coke	Elefant (m)	Elephant

C

Cappuccino (m) (Gaputschino)	Cappuccino	Consierge (m) (Gonsiersch)	Concierge	Elektrogschäft (n)	Electrical shop
		cool	cool (kuul)	elf	eleven
		Cousin (m) (Gusän)	Cousin		

Elterähuus (n)	Parent's home
Empfang (m)	Reception
energisch	vigorous
entlang	along (prep)
entschuldigung	Excuse me
enttüscht	disappointed
Enzündig (f)	Infection
Erdbeeri (n)	Strawberry
Erdnussbutter (m)	Peanut butter
erscht	first
erschtä Schtokk	first floor
Erschti Hilf (f)	First Aid
erschtunt	amazed
Erwachsenä/i (m/f)	Adult
Eschtrich (m)	Attic
Esel (m)	Donkey
Espresso (m)	Expresso
Essig (m)	Vinegar
Event (m) (iwent)	Event
exgüsi	Excuse me

F

Faanä (f)	Flag
Faaruuswis (m)	Driver's licence
fad	tasteless
Fäld (n)	Field
Faltä	fold (verb)
Familiäschluuch (m)	Family get- together
Familiäschtand (m)	Marital status
Familiäzämäkunft (f)	Family get- together
Fänschter (n)	Window
fantastisch	fantastic
Fäscht (n)	Party
Fasnacht (f)	Carnival
Februar (m)	February
Felchä (f)	White fish
Feriä (pl)	Vacations
Fernbediänig (f)	Remote control
Fernse (n)	Television
Fernsebewilligung (f)	Television licence
feschthebä	grap (verb)
Fiäber (n)	Fever
Finger (m)	Finger
Fingernagel (m)	Fingernail
Finkä (pl)	Slippers
Fisch (m)	Fish
fischä	fish (verb)
Fitness	Fitness
Fitnessruum (m)	Gym
Flaisch (n)	Meat
Flügä (f)	Fly
Flugzüg (n)	Aeroplane
Flugzüg-Tikket (n)	Flight ticket
flüschterä	whisper (verb)
Fluss (m)	River
Flusspferd (n)	Hippopotamus
föif	five
Föön (m)	Foehn
Forälä (f)	Trout
Formular (n)	Form

forwardä	forward (verb)
Foti (n)	Photo
Frau (f)	Wife
frei	vacant
fridlich (slang)	peaceful
Friitig	Friday
frittiert	deep fried
Frölain (n)	young woman
froo	joyful
fröölich	cheerful
früä	early
Früälig (m)	Spring
Frucht (f)	Fruit
Fründ/in (m/f)	Friend
früsch	fresh
Fuäss (m)	Foot
Fuchs (m)	Fox
Füdli (n)	Bottom
füecht	humid
füft	fifth
füfzä	fifteen
füfzg	fifty
für	for (prep)
Füür (n)	Fire

G

gääl	yellow
gäänä	yawn (verb)
Gablä (f)	Fork
gaga	crazy
gägä	against (prep), into (prep)
Gägägift (n)	Antidote
gägänüber	across from (prep)
gägänüber	opposite (prep)
Gägäwart (f)	Present
Gaiss (f)	Goat
Gäld (n)	Money
Gäld inweschtierä	invest money
Gäld verdiänä	earn money
Gäldautomat (m)	Cash machine
Gäldüberwiisig (f)	Postal money order
gämblä	to gamble
Gämsi (f)	Chamois
Gang (m)	Hallway
Garage (f) (Garasch)	Garage
Gardäröbä (f)	Wardrobe
Gartä (m)	Garden
Gebäkk (n)	Pastry
Geboide (n)	Building
Gebür (f)	Fee
Geburtstags-party (f)	Birthday party
gedigä (slang)	comfortable
geimä	to play
Genemigung (f)	Permit
Geografii (f)	Geography
Gepäkk (n)	Luggage
geschter	Yesterday
Ghaimnummerä (f)	Code (secret)
Ghirnerschütterig (f)	Concussion

ghörä	hear (verb)
Gift (n)	Poison
giggerig	horny
Gipfel (m)	Peak
Gipfeli (n)	Croissant
git	equals
gkocht	boiled
Glacé (n) (Glasse)	Ice cream
Glais (n)	Track
glangwiilet	bored
Glas (n)	Glass
Glüäwii (m)	hot wine
glükklich	happy
Glükkszaal (f)	lucky number
Gmüäs (n)	Vegetables
gmüätlich	cosy
gold	gold (colour)
Gomfi (f)	Jam
görpsä	burp (verb)
görpslä (Babys)	burp (verb)
gradi Zaalä	even numbers
graduus	straight on
Gränzä (f)	Border
Gränzä (f)	Frontier
Grapefruitsaft (m) (Gräpfrüsaft)	Grapefruit juice
grau	grey
Grawattä (f)	Tie
griiffä	grap (verb)
griliert	grilled
Grill (m)	Grill
Grillfäscht (n)	Barbecue
Grippe (f)	Flu
Gros-chind (n)	Grandchild
gröschtet	roasted
Groselterä (pl)	Grandparents
Grosmuetter (f)	Grandmother
gross	big, large
Grostantä (f)	Great aunt
Grosunggle (m)	Great uncle
Grosvatter (m)	Grandfather
grüän	green
Grüezi	Hello
Gschäft (n)	Business
gschidä	divorced
Gschirr (n)	Dishes
Gschmakk (m)	Flavour
gschmakklos	tasteless
gschtresst	stressed
Gschwindigkaitsbegränzig (f)	Speed limit
Gschwüschterti (pl)	Siblings
gsee	see
Gsellschaft (f)	Society
Gsicht (n)	Face
guet	good
Güggel (m)	Rooster
gumpä	jump (verb)
Gurt (m)	Belt
Gürtel (m)	Belt

Dictionary

gwagglä	wiggle (verb)	Hummer (m)	Lobster
Gwitter (n)	Thunderstorm	Humoor (m)	Humour
Gwürz (pl)	Condiment	Hund (m)	Dog

H

		hundert	hundred
		hunderttuusig	hundred thousand
Haanä (m)	Faucet/ tap	Hunger (m)	hungry
Haar (pl)	Hair	Husiweiigs-party (f)	Housewarming
Hagel (m)	Hail	hüt	Today
haglä	hail (verb)	hüüla	cry (verb)
Hailmittel (n)	Medicine	Huusgloggä (f)	Doorbell
haimelig	cosy	Huusnummerä (f)	House number
haiss	hot	Huut (f)	Skin
haissi Milch (f)	hot milk		
haissi Schoggi (f)	hot chocolate		

I

halal	halal	Ichaufszentrum (n)	Shopping centre
halb durä	medium (meat)	ifersüchtig	jealous
Halbpension (f)	Half board	igschribnä Briäf (m)	Registered letter
Hals (m)	Throat	igschribni Poscht (f)	Registered mail
hammer (slang)	super	iichauffä	shop (verb)
Hämp (n)	Shirt	Iichaufs-Täschä (f)	Shopping bag
Hand (f)	Hand	Iigang (m)	Entrance
Handcreme (f) (Hand-gräm)	Hand cream	Iigangshallä (f)	Entry way
		Iikomä (n)	Income
Händi(n)	Mobile phone	iiloggä	log in (verb)
Handörgeli (n)	Swiss accordion	iiraisä	immigrate (verb)
Händtröchner (m)	Hand dryer	Iis-tee (m)	Iced tea
Häntschä (pl)	Gloves	iitschäggä	check in (verb)
Härd (m)	Stove	in	in (prep), into (prep)
Härpscht (m)	Autumn	Inland-Nachrichtä(pl)	National news
Härz (n)	Heart	Insekt (n)	Insect
härzig	lovely	Inslä (f)	Island
hässig	furious	Intensivschtazion (f)	Intensive care
Hauptschpiis (f)	Main course	internazionalä Aaruäf (m)	long distance call
hebä	hold (verb)		
Hecht (m)	Pike	Inweschtierig (f)	Investment
Heftli (n)	Magazine	Inweschtizion (f)	Investment
hell	light	irgendöppis	anything
Herdöpfel (m)	Potatoes	irgendwiä	somehow
Herusgeber/in (m/f)	Editor	irr	crazy
hetero(sexuell)	heterosexual	isch glich	equals
Hilfe (f)	help		
Himbeeri (n)	Raspberry		

J

hinder	behind (prep)	ja	yes
Hinderlegig (f)	Deposit (money)	Jaar (n)	Year
Hirsch (m)	Deer	Jaaresziit (f)	Season
Hizz (f)	Heat	Jaarhundert (n)	Century
Hochziit (f)	Wedding	Jaartuusig (n)	Millennium
Hoi	Hi (informal)	Jagge (f)	Jacket
Hoi zäme	Hi (to several)	Januar (m)	January
Hoischnuppä (m)	Hay fever	Jeans (pl) (Tschins)	Jeans
homo(sexuell)	homosexual	jezt	present, now
Honig (m)	Honey	Job (m) (Tschop)	Occupation
Hosä (f)	Trousers	Jobbeschribig (f)	Job description
Huän (n)	Chicken	jodlä	yodel (verb)
Huänerhuut (f)	Goose bumps	Joghurt (n) (Jogurt)	Yoghurt
huäschtä	cough (verb)	Juli (m)	July
Huät (m)	Hat	jungä Maa (m)	young man
Hüft (f)	Hip	jungi Frau (f)	young woman
Hügel (m)	Hill	Juni (m)	June
Hülsäfrücht (pl)	Legumes	Jupe (m) (Schüpp)	Skirt

K

Kabelfernse (n)	Cable TV
Kafi (crème) (m)	Coffee with cream
Kafi (n)	Coffee bar / cafe
Kafichränzli (n)	Coffee party
Kafiklatsch (m)	Coffee party
Kafipausä (f)	Coffee break
Kakerlakä (f)	Cockroach
Kanal (m)	Channel
känslä	cancel (verb)
Kantinä (f)	Canteen
Kanton (m)	County
Kassierer/in (m/f)	Cashier
Katedraale (f)	Cathedral
Kino (n)	Cinema
Klatsch (m)	Gossip
klatschä	gossip (verb)
Klima (n)	Climate
Klinik (f)	Clinic
Kod (m)	Code
Komission (f)	Commission
Kondom (n)	Condom
Konfäränz (f)	Conference
Kontinänt (m)	Continent
Konzärt (n)	Concert
kopierä	copy (verb)
Körperlozioon (f)	Body lotion
koscher	kosher
Koschtüm (n)	Suit (for woman)
Krabä (f)	Crab
Kreditchartä (f)	Credit card
Krokodil (n)	Crocodile
Kultur (f)	Culture
Kunscht (f)	Art
Kurs (m)	Course
küssä	kiss (verb)
kuul (slang)	Cool

L

Läbäs-Partner/in (m/f)	Partner (love)
Läbere (f)	Liver
Läbesmittel (pl)	Groceries
Labor (n)	Laboratory
lachä	laugh (verb)
lächlä	smile
Lachs (m)	Salmon
Ladä (m)	Shop
Ladä (m)	Store
lädälä	shopping (go)
Läder (n)	Leather
Lagerhallä (f)	Warehouse
Laischtigsbewärtig (f)	Appraisal
Lamm (n)	Lamb
Land (n)	Country
landä	land (verb)
lang	long
langärmlig	long sleeves
Laptop (m) (Läptop)	Laptop
läsä	read (verb)

Dictionary

Latte Macchiato (f) (Maggiato)	Latte Macchiato	Meeresfrücht (pl)	Seafood	Necessaire (n) (Nessessär)	Toiletry bag
Lavabo (n)	Washbasin	Meersoili (n)	Guinea pig	Nichtä (f)	Niece
Lawinä (f)	Avalanche	mega (slang)	super	niidisch	envious
ledig	single	Mensa (f)	Canteen	Nilpferd (n)	Hippopotamus
Leerling (m)	Apprentice	merci (märsi)	thank you	Noibau (m)	Building (new)
lesbisch	lesbian	Mezzg (f)	Butcher's shop	noimät	somewhere
liäbä	love (verb)	Mieter/in (m/f)	Tenant	Notfall (m)	Emergency
Lift (m)	Lift	Mietwonig (f)	Rental flat	Notufnaam (f)	Emergency room
Liibli (n)	T-Shirt	Mikrowälä (f)	Microwave	Novämber (m)	November
Liinä (f)	Linen	Milch (f)	Milk	null	zero
lila	Lilac	Milchkafi (m)	Coffee with milk	nün	nine
Limone (f)	Lime	mild	mild	nünt	ninth
linggs	left	Milliard (f)	billion	nünzä	nineteen
Linsä (pl)	Lentils	Million (f)	million	nünzg	ninety
Löffel (m)	Spoon	Mineralwasser (n)	Mineral water	nüt	nothing
Loi (m)	Lion	minus	minus	Nylon (n) (Nailon)	Nylon
lokale Aaruäf (m)	Local call	Minutä (f)	Minute		
lokali Nachrichtä (pl)	Local news	mit	by(prep), with(prep)	**O**	
lokali Noiigkaitä (pl)	Local news	Mittag (m)	Noon/ midday		
Loon (m)	Salary	Mittagspausä (f)	Lunch break	Oberschinä (f)	Eggplant
losä	listen (verb)	mittleri Grössi	medium (size)	oberschti Schtokk (m)	Top floor
löschä	cancel (verb)	Mittwuch	Wednesday	Obertail (n)	Top
luägä	look (verb)	Modä (f)	Fashion	Ofä (m)	Oven
luägä	watch (verb)	Moisebussard (m)	Buzzard	öffentlichs Telefon (n)	Public telephone
Luchs (m)	Lynx	Momänt (m)	moment	Oktober (m)	October
Luftposcht (f)	Airmail	Monät (m)	Month	Olivenöl (n)	Olive oil
Luftschuzzchäller (m)	Bunker	Mönggi (n) (slang)	Idiot	ooni	without
Lungebröötli(n)(slang)	Cigarette	Morgä (m)	Morning	Oor (n)	Ear
luschtig	funny	Morgädämmerig (f)	Dawn	Operä (f)	Opera
lutschä	lick (verb)	morn	Tomorrow	Operazion (f)	Operation
		Moschee (f)	Mosque	Öpfel (m)	Apple
M		mozzä (slang)	complain (verb)	Öpfelsaft (m)	Apple juice
		müäd	sleepy	öpper	somebody
Maa (m)	Husband	Muetter (f)	Mother	öppis	something
Määl (n)	Flour	Muggä (f)	Mosquito	orangsch	orange (colour)
Maalzitä (pl)	Meals	Mumeltiär (n)	Marmot	Orangschä (f)	Orange
Magä (m)	Stomach	Münz (n)	Change (money)	Orangschägomfi (f)	Marmalade
Mai (m)	May	Münzä (f)	Coin	Orangschäsaft (m)	Orange juice
Mainig (f)	Opinion	Museum (n)	Museum	O-Saft (m)	Orange juice
Mais (m)	Corn	Musig (f)	Music	Ozean (m)	Ocean
Mais-cholbä (m)	Corn on the cob	Müsli (n)	Mouse		
Mait(ä)li (n)	Girl	Muul (n)	Mouth	**P**	
Maitli (n)	Baby girl	Muus (f)	Mouse		
mälchä	milk (verb)			Päch (n)	Bad luck
Manager/in (m/f)(Mänätscher/in)	Manager	**N**		Päkkli (n)	Packet
Mandarinli (n)	Tangerine	näbäd	beside (prep), next	Papiertuäch (n)	Paper towel
mängisch	sometimes	Näbel (m)	Fog	Parasit (m)	Parasite
Mantel (m)	Coat	nach	according to (prep)	Pariserbrot (n)	Baguette
Mäntig	Monday	nach	after (prep)	Park (m)	Park
Marder (m)	Marten	Nachbarä (pl)	Neighbours	Parkplazz (m)	Parking area
Margerinä (f)	Margarine	Nachrichtä (pl)	The news	Partär (n)	Ground floor
mariniert	marinated	Nacht (f)	Night	Partner/in (m/f)	Partner
Markä (f)	Brand, Stamp	Näffä (m)	Nephew	Party (f) (Parti)	Party
März (m)	March	Nagel (m)	Nail	Pass (m)	Passport
Märzetüpfli (pl)	Freckles	nai	no	Passaschiir (m)	Passenger
Massage (f) (Masaasch)	Massage	Nakkä (f)	Neck	Pasta (f)	Pasta
Mässer (n)	Knife	Namittag (m)	Afternoon	Pausä (f)	Break
mee	more	Nasä (f)	Nose	Paziänt/in (m/f)	Patient
Meer (n)	Sea	Nashorn (n)	Rhinoceros	Penis (m)	Penis
		Natel (n)	Mobile phone	Pensionskassä (f)	Pension fund
				Pepperoni (f)	Pepper

Dictionary

Perron (n)	Platform	Rauchereggä (m)	Smoking area	Schlafzimmer (n)	Bedroom
Pfanä (f)	Pan	redä	speak (verb)	Schlagzilä (pl)	Headlines
Pflägfachfrau (f)	Nurse	reduziert	Discount	Schlangä (f)	Snake
Pflägfachmaa (m)	Nurse	Ree (n)	Roe deer	schlapp	sleepy
Pfläschterli (n)	Band-aid	Reschtorant (m)	Restaurant	schlöfrig	sleepy
Pissoir (n) (Pissuar)	Urinal	Resepzionischt/in (m/f)	Receptionist	Schlüssel (m)	Key
Plan (m)	Plan	reserviärä	reserve (verb)	Schmärzä (pl)	Pain
plus	plus	Rezäpt (n)	Prescription	schmärzhaft	painful
Polteraabig (m)	Wedding eve's party	Rezepzion (f)	Reception	Schmärzmittel (n)	Pain Killer
Polteraabig (m)	Hen night	Riis (m)	Rice	Schminkzüg (n)	Make-up
Polyester (m)	Polyester	Riisecrevettä (f) (Riiság-	Prawns	schmökkä	smell
Poscht (f)	Post	röwettä)		Schnägg (m)	Slug
Poscht (f)	Post office	Rindflaisch (n)	Beef	schnäll	hurry
poschtä	buy (verb)	Rokk (m)	Skirt	Schnaps (m)	Spirit
Poschtchartä (f)	Postcard	roo	raw	Schnee (m)	Snow
Poschtlaitzaal (f)	Postcode	rosa	pink	Schnugi	sweetie
Pöschtler/in (m/f)	Postman	Ross (n)	Horse	schön	beautiful
Poschtschtämpfel (m)	Postage stamp	rot	red	schpaat	late
Poulet (n) (Pule)	Chicken	Rotä (m)	Red wine	Schpäkk (m)	Bacon
Praktikant/in (m/f)	Trainee	Rotwii (m)	Red wine	schparä	save (verb)
Präsentazion (f)	Presentation	Rüäbli (n)	Carrots	Schparkonto (n)	Savings account
Praxis (f)	Doctor's surgery	Ruggä (m)	Back	Schpiägel (m)	Mirror
Pricht (m)	Report	Rukksakk (m)	Rucksack	Schpiil (n)	Game
Priis (m)	Fee , Price	Ruum (m)	Space	Schpiiswagä (m)	Dining car
Profi (m)	Professional			schpilä	to gamble, to play
Profit (m)	Profit			Schpinä (f)	Spider
Promi (m)	Celebrity	Sach (f)	Thing	Schpinat (m)	Spinach
Proscht	Cheers	sächs	six	Schpital (n)	Hospital
Pröschtli	Cheers	sächst	sixth	schpizz	horny
prötlet	fried	sächzä	sixteen	Schport (m)	Sports
Protokoll (n)	Minutes	sächzg	sixty	Schprüzzä (f)	Injection
Pruäf (m)	Occupation	Saft (m)	Juice	Schtaat (m)	State
Pschtekk (n)	Cutlery	Salami (m)	Salami	Schtadt (f)	Town, City
pschtelä	order (verb)	Salär (n)	Salary	Schtadtplan (m)	City map
Pschtellig (f)	Purchase order	Salat (m)	Salad	Schtägä (f)	Stairs
psezt	engaged	Salatsossä (f)	Dressing	Schtaibokk (m)	European ibex
Psizzer/in (m/f)	Owner	Sali	Hi (informal)	Schtangä (f)	Draft beer
Pult (n)	Desk	Salü	Hi (informal)	schtarrä	stare (verb)
Punsch (m)	Punch	salzig	salty	Schtazion(f)	Ward
Pürli (n)	Roll	sammlä	collect (verb)	Schtekker (m)	Plug
Purscht (m)	young man	Samschtig	Saturday	Schtiär (m)	Bull
Puzzma/frau (m/f)	Cleaner	sändä	send (verb)	Schtirn (f)	Forehead
		Sandwich (m) (Sänd-	Sandwich	Schträäl (m)	Comb
		witsch)		Schtrand (m)	Beach
Quali(fikation) (f)	Appraisal	Satellit (m)	Satellite	Schtrass (f)	Street
Quark (m)	Curd cheese	Satellitäschüsslä (f)	Satellite Dish	Schtriit (m)	Argument
		Sau (f)	Pig	schtriitä	argue (verb)
		Schachtlä (f)	Box	Schtrümpf (pl)	Stockings
Raam (m)	Cream	Schad!	What a shame!	Schtuäl (m)	Chair
Rächnig (f)	Invoice	Schal (m)	Scarf	Schtubä (f)	Lounge
rächts	right	Schalä (f)	Coffee with milk	Schtudio (n)	Studio
Radar (m)	Speed camera	Schalter (m)	Counter	Schtund (f)	Hour
Radio (m)	Radio	Schampoo (n)	Shampoo	Schtürä (pl)	Taxes
Räge (m)	Rain	scharf	spicy	Schturm (m)	Storm
Rappä (m)	Rappen	Schegg (m)	Cheque	Schuä (pl)	Shoes
Rasä (m)	Lawn	schikkä	send (verb)	Schuäl (f)	School
Rasämäier (m)	Lawnmower	Schildchrot (f)	Turtle	Schubladä (f)	Drawer
Raschtplazz (m)	Service area	Schinkä (m)	Ham	schüch	shy
Raschtschtettä (f)	Service area	schlächt	bad	Schulterä (f)	Shoulder
Rasiärklingä (f)	Razor blades	Schlaflosikait (f)	Insomnia	Schüsslä (f)	Bowl

Section headers: **Q**, **R**, **S**

Dictionary

schüttlä	shake (verb)	Tail (m)	Section	Turischt/in (m/f)	Tourist
Schwager (m)	Brother-in-law	tailziit	Part time	tüür	expensive
Schwaineflaisch (n)	Pork	Take away (m) (Teik Awei)	Take away	Tüür (f)	Door
schwarz	black			tuusig	thousand
Schwigermuetter (f)	Mother-in-law	Talk Show (f) (Tok Schou)	Talk show		
Schwigersoon (m)	Son-in-law				
Schwigertochter (f)	Daughter-in-law	Täller (m)	Plate	über	above (prep)
Schwigervatter (m)	Father -in-law	Talliä (f)	Waist	über	across (prep)
Schwiizer Frankä (m)	Swiss Francs	Tankschtell (f)	Petrol station	über	over (prep)
schwingä	Swiss wrestling	Tantä (f)	Aunt	überrascht	surprised
Schwinigs (n)	Pork	tanzä	dance (verb)	Überschtundä (pl)	Overtime
Schwö(schter) (f)	Sister	Täschä (f)	Bag	überwiisä	transfer (verb)
Schwögerin (f)	Sister-in-law	Tassä (f)	Cup	uf	on (horiz.surface) (prep)
schwul	gay	Techniker/in (m/f)	Technician	Uf widerluägä	Bye
schwümä	to swim	Tee (m)	Tea	Uf widersee!	Bye
Schwümmbad (n)	Swimming pool	Teelöffeli (n)	Teaspoon	ufä	up
See (m)	Lake	Teeni (m) (Tiini)	Teenager	Ufenthaltsgenemi- gung(f)	Residence permit
Sekretär/in (m/f)	Secretary	Telefonbeantworter (m)	Answering machine		
Sekundä (f)	second	Telefonbuäch (n)	Telephone book	um	around (prep)
sentimental	sentimental	Telefonchartä (f)	Telephone card	umarmä	hug (verb)
Septämber (m)	September	Telefonnummerä (f)	Phone number	und	plus (maths)
Serviettä (f)	Napkin	Telefonrächnig (f)	Telephone bill	under	beneath (prep), under (prep)
sexy	sexy	Temperatur (f)	Temperature		
Shorts (pl)	Shorts	Tennisschuä (pl)	Tennis Shoes	Undergschoss (n)	Basement
sibä	seven	Teppich (m)	Carpet	Underhosä (f)	Panties
sibät	seventh	Termin (m)	Appointment	Underwösch (f)	Underwear
sibäzg	seventy	Terrassä (f)	Terrace	Unggle (m)	Uncle
sibzä	seventeen	Theater (n)	Theatre	Unglükkszaal (f)	unlucky number
sich tränä	separate (verb)	Thema (n)	Subject	ungradi Zaalä	odd numbers
Sicherhait (f)	Security	Tiger (m)	Tiger	Uniform (f)	Uniform
Sidä (f)	Silk	Tisch (m)	Table	Unterhaltig (f)	Entertainment
silber	silver (colour)	Tischmattä (f)	Table mats	Unterschrift (f)	Signature
single	single	Tischset (n)	Dinner service	unzwungä	Business casual
Sizzig (f)	Meeting	Tischtuäch (n)	Table cloth	Urgrosmuetter (f)	Great grandmother
SMS (n) (Äsämäs)	Text message	Tochter (f)	Daughter	Urgrosvatter (m)	Great grandfather
so so (la la)	so-so	Todesaazaig (f)	Obituary	us	from (prep)
Soiffä (f)	Soap	Toilettä (f) (Tualettä)	Toilet	Ussländer/in (m/f)	Foreigner
Sokkä (pl)	Socks	Tollwuät (f)	Rabies	Ussland-Nachrichtä (pl)	International news
Soon (m)	Son	Tomatä (f)	Tomato	uufgreggt	excited
sorry	sorry	Ton (m)	Tuna	Uuftrag (m)	Purchase order
Steak (n) (Steik)	Steak	Tooscht (m)	Toast	uusgä	spend (verb)
süäss	sweet	trännt	separated	uusloggä	log out (verb)
Süässmoscht (m)	Apple juice	Tratsch (m)	Gossip	uusraisä	emigrate (verb)
sugä	suck (verb)	Traveller cheques(pl) (Träwälär Schegg)	Travellers'cheque	Uus-schtellig (f)	Exposition
Summer (m)	Summer			uuströchnä	dry out (verb)
Sunä (f)	Sun	trochä	dry	uus-tschäggä	check out (verb)
Sunätach (n)	Sunshade	Tröpfli (pl)	Drops	Uusverchauff	Sale (rebate)
sunig	sunny	Truthaan (m)	Turkey	uusziä	move out (verb)
Sunntig	Sunday	Truubesaft (m)	Grape juice		
Supermärt (m)	Supermarket	truurig	sad		
suur	sour	Tschüss	Bye (informal)	Vagina (f)	Vagina
suurä Moscht (m)	Cider	tschutä	play football(verb)	Vatter (m)	Father
		T-Shirt (n)	T-Shirt	vegan(isch)	vegan
		Tuäch (n)	Scarf	vegetarisch	vegetarian
Taal (n)	Valley	Tüächli (n)	Towel	Verband (m)	Bandage
Tach (n)	Roof	Tüfchüäler (m)	Freezer	Verbilligung (f)	Discounts
Tachrinnä (f)	Gutters	Tüfgarasch (f)	Basement garage	Verbindig (f)	Connection
Tachwonig (f)	Attic flat	tüfgfrorä	frozen	verbränä	burn (verb)
Tag (m)	Day	Tumbler (m) (Tömbler)	Tumble drier	verchauffä	sell (verb)
Taigwarä (pl)	Pasta	Turi (m) (slang)	Tourist	Vercheltig (f)	Cold

Verchoiffer/in (m/f)	Salesperson	Warum?	Why?
vergangä	past	Was ?	What ?
Vergangähait (f)	Past	wäschä	wash (verb)
vergiftet	poisoned	Wäschpi (n)	Wasp
Verhüetigsmittel (n)	Contraceptive	Wasser mit Cholesüüri	Water with gas
verhüratet	married	Wasser ooni Cholesüüri	Water without gas
Verlezzig (f)	Injury	Wassermelonä (f)	Watermelon
verlobt	engaged	Wätter (n)	Weather
Verlobtä (m)	Fiancé	Wätterpricht (m)	Forecast
Verlobti (f)	Fiancée	Wätterpricht (m)	Weather report
Verluscht (m)	Loss	WC (n) (Weze)	Toilet
Vermieter/in (m/f)	Landlord	WC-Papier (n) (Weze-	Toilet paper
Vermittlig (f)	Operator	Papier)	
verrukkt	crazy	Wekkaaruäf (m)	Wake up call
Verschpötig (f)	Delay	wenig	few
Versicherig (f)	Insurance	weniger	less
Versicherigsnummerä(f)	Insurance number	Wiä?	How?
Vertailer (m)	Digestive	Wii (m)	Wine
Vertrag (m)	Contract	wiiss	white
Verwaltig (f)	Estate agency	Wiissä (m)	White wine
Verwaltigsrat (m)	Board of Directors	Wiissbrot (n)	White bread
Verwandti (pl)	Relatives	Wiisswii (m)	White wine
verwitwet	widowed	wiit	wide
verzollä	declare (verb)	wiiterlaitä	forward (verb)
verzwiiflet	desperate	wiitsichtig	long-sighted
vier	four	Wildsau (f)	Wild boar
viert	fourth	Willkomä	Welcome
vierzä	fourteen	Wimperä (pl)	Eyelash
vierzg	forty	Wind (m)	Wind
vill	many , much	Wind sörfä	Wind Surfing
violett	violet	Windä (f)	Attic
VIP (m) (Wiaipi)	Celebrity	Winter (m)	Winter
vo	from (prep)	Wirus (m)	Virus
vo	of (prep)	Wisum (n)	Visa
Vogel (m)	Bird	Witwe (f)	Widow
Vollkornbrot (n)	Whole grain bread	Witwer (m)	Widower
Vollpension (f)	Full board	Wizz (m)	Joke
vollziit	Full time	wizzig	funny
vor	in front of (prep)	Wo?	Where?
Vorhallä (f)	Lobby	Wohi?	Where to?
Vorhäng (pl)	Curtains	Wolf (m)	Wolf
Vorruum (m)	Lobby	wolkig	cloudy
Vorschpiis (f)	Starter	Wösch (f)	Laundry
Vorwaal (f)	Area code	Wöschchuchi (f)	Laundry room
		Wöschmaschine (f)	Washing machine

W

Waag (f)	Scales	Wöschmittel (n)	Detergent
Wäärig (f)	Currency	Wöschplan (m)	Laundry schedule
Wächselratä (f)	Exchange rate	Wöschsakk (m)	Laundry bag
Wäg (m)	Footpath	Wöschtag (m)	Laundry day
Wäg (m)	Path	Wuchä (f)	Week
Wäjä (f)	Pie	Wuchänänd (n)	Weekend
Wald (m)	Forest	Wulä (f)	Wool
Wält (f)	World	Wurm (m)	Worm
Wänn?	When?	Wurscht (f)	Sausage
Wanzä (f)	Bug		
Wär?	Who?		
Warähuus (n)	Warehouse		
Wärbig (f)	Advertising		
warm	warm		

Z

zä	ten
Zaa (m)	Tooth
Zaabürschteli (n)	Toothbrush
Zaapaschtä (f)	Toothpaste

Zaine (f)	Laundry basket
Zäjä (m)	Toe
Zäjänagel (m)	Toenail
zalä	pay (verb)
Zalig (f)	Payment
Zältli (n)	Candy
Zander (m)	Jack salmon
zät	tenth
zaubärä	magic, to do (verb)
Zauberai (f)	Magic
Zebra (n)	Zebra
zfridä	joyful
Ziischtig	Tuesday
Zimmer (n)	Room
Zimmerservice(m) (Zim-	Room service
mer-Serwis)	
Zins (m)	Interest
Zitig (f)	Newspaper
Zitrone (f)	Lemon
Zmittag (m)	Lunch
Zmittagässä (n)	Lunch
Zmorgä (m)	Breakfast
Znacht (m)	Dinner
Znachtassä (n)	Dinner
Znüni (m)	Snack (morning)
Zoll (m)	Customs
Zoo (m)	Zoo
zruggschriibä	reply (verb)
zu	to (prep)
zuähebä	cover (verb)
Zuäkumft (f)	Future
zuäkümftig	Future
Zug (m)	Train
Zugbilet (n)	Train ticket
zuhandä vo	Care of
Zukker (m)	Sugar
Zungä (f)	Tongue
Zvieri (m)	Snack (afternoon)
zwai	two
zwaihundert	two hundred
zwait	second
zwaituusig	two thousand
Zwaizimmerwonig (f)	Two-room apt.
zwänzg	twenty
Zwiblä (f)	Onion
Zwilling (pl)	Twins
zwinkerä	wink (verb)
zwölf	twelve
zwüschä	between (prep)

(DÄ SCHLUSS)

The End

(SOODELI, DAS WÄÄRS)

Dictionary

Index

About the Authors

S ergio is a Colombian-Anglo-Swiss author, brought up in the fresh surroundings of his family's 'Hacienda', a coffee plantation somewhere in the Colombian Andes. After earning a BA as an economist, he worked in this field for more than 12 years in Colombia, Spain and the UK.

However, seeking to challenge his economist side, he studied comics and illustration at the Joso Comic School in Barcelona, where he developed his talent for cartooning.

He is the author of *"Switzerland a cartoon survival guide", "Colombia a Comedy of Errors"* (Amazon Bestseller)and *"La Indispensable Novena de Aguinaldos"*. He is also an editorial cartoonist and has published his cartoons and comic strips in newspapers and magazines in Switzerland.

Sergio is constantly working on his future books, as well as illustrating and designing for several international companies in Europe. As he says: "… It's all about having fun!..".

N icole Egger was born and grew up in Zurich. She received her master's in linguistics and literature from the University of Zurich. During her studies she taught German and Swiss German to the increasingly international community in Switzerland. After her degree she changed her career and has been working in the communication industry.

Having lived abroad, including a year in Beijing to study Chinese, she sympathizes with newcomers to Switzerland who are confronted with a difficult, funny-sounding language. She is perceptive to the difficulties that students may encounter. But her real challenge is to encourage people who are learning a foreign language to become confident and competent in a way that is still fun.

Acknowledgements

Many people have helped in many ways to make this book a reality. They have given us their time and knowledge to help this book be amusing and useful. To all of them our sincere gratitude. In particular we would like to mention:

Anja Kauf, Richard Harvell, Dianne Dicks, Claudia Holenstein, Michael Landolt, Roberto Lievano, Miguel Lievano, Manuel Kauf, Victoria Kellaway, Marcel Untersander, Ingrid Larsen, Hsiang–Yun Tseng, André Klauser and David Pybus.

The Hoi Family

our editions of the singular, best-selling Swiss German survival guide

Hoi – your new Swiss German survival guide *by* Sergio J. Lievano and Nicole Egger (Swiss German / Zurich dialect – English edition). ISBN 978-3-905252-67-5.

Hoi et après... Manuel de survie en suisse allemand *by Sergio J. Lievano and Nicole Egger.* (Zurich dialect - French edition of Hoi) ISBN 978-3-905252-16-3.

Sali zämme – your Baseldütsch survival guide *by Sergio J. Lievano and Nicole Egger.* Basel dialect ISBN 978-3-905252-26-2.

Hoi Zäme – Schweizerdeutsch leicht gemacht *von Sergio J. Lievano und Nicole Egger* macht mit seinen über 200 witzigen und farbenfrohen Cartoons das Erlernen der Sprache zu einem vergnüglichen Erlebnis. (*Hoi Zäme* is the Swiss German (Zurich dialect) – High German edition of Hoi) ISBN 978-3-905252-22-4.

AND NOW...

THE
INDISPENSABLE
ILLUSTRATED
DICTIONARY
TO SWISS
GERMAN

A companion dictionary to the best-selling swiss german guide of all time

Finally, an easy way to learn Swiss German: with pictures. This book features more than 3000 of the most important Swiss German words—as well as some of the most entertaining and most misunderstood!

Written phonetically for easy comprehension, the vocabulary in this book is a great introduction to Switzerland's most-spoken dialect. Use it on its own, or in combination with *Hoi—your Swiss German survival guide.*